Don't Kiss Me Goodbye! I'm Going With You.

A collection of
previously published
newspaper columns,
magazine articles
and fiction.

Don't Kiss Me Goodbye! I'm Going With You.

Patricia Costa Viglucci

PATRI PUBLICATIONS

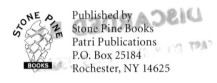

Published by
Stone Pine Books
Patri Publications
P.O. Box 25184
Rochester, NY 14625

Book Layout and Cover Design by John Costa Viglucci, GT Grafix
Cover Photo by Patricia Costa Viglucci

Manufactured in the United States of America

ISBN: 0-964591456

DON'T KISS *ME* GOODBYE!
I'M GOING WITH YOU.
A collection of previously published newspaper columns,
magazine articles and other essays and stories.

by Patricia Costa Viglucci

Family, Children, Travel, Humor, Recipes

Please address all inquiries to:
Stone Pine Books
Patri Publications
P.O. Box 25184
Rochester, NY 14625

Dedication

*For my husband Carmen and our children
Johanna, John and Cara who unwittingly
provided more fodder than could ever be utilized.*

*And, for the "beloved bears" found at the end of this book
who continue creatively in their parents' footsteps.*

Acknowledgments

Much love and many thanks to:

Our creative son, John Costa Viglucci, a graphic artist,
who grapples with the jumble of pages I send him,
and who always produces a beautiful book.

My husband Carmen, who began editing my work at the Democrat
and Chronicle some 40 years ago, and continues to this day—
and whose judgment I value above all others.

Ron Bartlett, son-in-law extraordinaire, illustrator of Upon a
Winter's Night, who has come to the rescue over the years
in more matters and more times than I can count.

Daughters Johanna and Cara and daughter-in-law Victoria, whose
support, love and encouragement in all matters, keeps us going.

Sisters Thomasina Costa Buonocore and Judith Costa Manza, my
best friends and confidantes, and without whose help the section
on family recipes would have been impossible to record.

Dear aunts, Madeline Borelli Leonard and Louise Borelli Gerardy,
for assistance in remembering the Conrad, Austin and
Roulette days, and coming up with family recipes.

Uncle Alfred Borelli, a kindred soul, whose writing inspires me.

Brothers Sam Costa and Paul Costa, creative cooks themselves,
who enjoy reminding me that of all the culinary artists
in the family hierarchy, I reside on the bottom rung.

Grandchildren, Tessa, Quinn, Riley, Austin, Samantha, Pierce,
Angel Jr. (A.J.), who make us laugh and fill our hearts with joy!

And always, The Paraclete.

Road Map

(Sometimes referred to as the Contents)

Introduction

When our first child came along, I quit my job as reporter and critic at the Rochester (N.Y.) Democrat and Chronicle to be a stay-at-home mom. I planned on fulfilling a long-held dream. I would take care of our dear baby's needs, then put her down to nap, while I would emulate Louisa Mae Alcott whose *Little Women* I first read at age eight, and which set me on the path to writing.

Reality set in right away. Our darling babe refused to cooperate. For the first six weeks I had no sleep, and was unable to write my name without help. When at the age of six weeks, Johanna suddenly began sleeping through the night, I had to deal with a condition for which I had no name. i.e., a state which hits working women suddenly cut off from their intellectual and social world. The zombie now became an anxiety-ridden zombie, and I dealt with depression. Eventually I regained my equilibrium, and began searching out weekly newspapers for which I could write a column about family life.

During my first job as women's editor at the Bradford (PA) *Era,* I wrote a weekly column titled *Kaffeeklatsch,* and focused on my birth family. But now with the additions of John and Cara, I had my own three children to write about. For nearly 40 years, I have chronicled their doings in Rochester suburban papers, The Catholic Courier Journal (using the pen name Sarah Child) and the Golden Times, along with other subjects which captured my attention. What follows is a random sampling along with some of the fiction and non-fiction published in magazines and newspapers over the years plus a few previously unpublished pieces.

Newspaper Columns

These columns were previously published starting in the mid-sixties in suburban Rochester newspapers in the Catholic Courier Journal, and most recently in the Golden Times of Rochester.

They are reprinted here, not necessarily in chronological order.

Taking Baby to Church

Some years ago, Louise, my same-age aunt, stood up during the sermon in St. Mary's, the small mission church in Roulette, Pa, and prepared to remove her irascible toddler who had been disturbing parishioners around them.

Without missing a beat, Fr. Regis Galvin, O.F.M, from nearby St. Bonaventure University, who'd been coming to say Mass for the last 20 years, stopped her in her tracks by noting to the glee of all but one, "That baby isn't bothering anybody. I can remember when you used to make more noise than that."

Champion cut-up in our family was my brother Sam. At age 2, Sam disappeared underneath the kneeler in the rear pew at St. Augustine's in Austin, Pa. where my parents were sitting and surfaced several minutes later in the front of the church, somewhat dusty from checking out the underpinnings of every pew in line.

Johanna, our oldest and a church goer from nine months of age, distinguished herself when the Communion bells rang out at her first time at Mass.

"Huddo," she yelled out in response to what sounded like the telephone.

All this came back to me a few weeks ago after attending a Mass in a small church outside Albany where we were visiting my mother-in-law in her new home. When she suggested she baby-sit and my husband and I go to church, I pooh poohed the idea.

"Come let's all go together. We don't see you that often.," then added, "If John (18 months) should act up, I can always go out with him."

And so we set out on a spring morning, the distance to the church so short that it was possible to walk, adding to our enjoyment of the day.

Once inside the church the enjoyment was short lived. John lasted for all of three minutes. He grew increasingly loud and by the time the young priest began delivering his sermon, John had started acting up accompanied by a sing-song libretto.

When the parishioners behind us began sighing and the little girl two seats in front of us turned around to stare, I sat tight. But my husband began to fidget. "Better get him out of here," he whispered. I stood up.

Without missing a beat, the curly-headed young priest commanded in stentorian tones, "Don't take that child out. It's not necessary."

I sat down, red-faced, muttering under my breath, "Good grief, Father, I wish you'd let me be the judge of that."

During the rest of the sermon as the priest's voice rose, so did John's. He sensed a contest. I pleaded softly, cajoled in vain. John dove head first out of my arms into the pew in front of us. Brought back, he twisted about in order to gabble to those behind us. Next he flirted with the little girl who was frowning at him. And when in frustration I squeezed his pudgy little leg somewhat harder than I might have, he squealed with every ounce of revenge he could muster.

At end of Mass I looked for the priest hoping to apologize, but he was nowhere in sight. But, I suspected he learned a little something about babies that day. Never, but never put them to the test.

(6/69)

Ever Watch A Tune-Car?

I've read the baby books along with everybody else. And I'm very much aware that the wise parent does not copy his child's baby talk when he is conversing with his offspring.

But it's a hard thing to do—particularly when the toddler comes up with a version that not only has more charm and music than anything Webster provides, but in its own way seems more apt than the staid and conventional dictionary usage.

Take, for example, that small square of terrycloth used for cleansing one's face and body.

When our daughter Johanna first started to utilize the language she christened it *wash closh*.

It seemed a perfect definition for the cold, soggy article usually found under the washbowl after she finished her morning ablutions.

Johanna added several other words to our family's vocabulary, most of them coined before she was two. Now, nearly five, she has improved her pronunciation as well as comprehension and no longer needs them to communicate. Her mother, however, to our daughter's amusement, still reverts to their use occasionally.

I cannot help myself. Grubby, the word she used to describe her mildly cranky condition upon waking from a nap, was more apt than "grumpy". She often did fall asleep with a little of the grime garnered from the morning's play and awoke the same way. Sometimes she arose from her nap both *grubby* and *wuggy* as anyone might be had they decided to skip lunch in favor of an extra 45 minutes in the sandbox.

Coffee, her mother's eyeopener, was *caw-caw* which sounds more like a picker-upper than the original label. Television was efficiently shortened to *tweshion* and the pasta dishes of which she was fond became a lilting *mackamoki.*

Her two-year-old brother John has coined his own words for the same objects. The TV to him is the *fifi.* His macaroni is shortened to *ronis.*

Jo's term of endearment *sweetheart* is *freetart* in her little brother's lexicon.

John excels in dubbing four-legged creatures. Spaniels are *puppy gogs* and both horses and cows are an economical *sorsy-cow.* Larger more frightening animals become *monkers.*

Trucks are *gucks* as anyone who has heard the grinding of gears knows and three-side geometric figures are *fryangles.* And those funny films the kids watch every Saturday morning? At your house they're cartoons. At ours, they're *tune-cars.*

(1/70)

Rigors of Vacation

"What! You're taking the children with you? What kind of vacation is that?" a friend wanted to know when we told her we were bound for Maine with the kids.

I didn't bother explaining we also eat supper with them every night, take them out to restaurants on occasion and on hot summer nights let them stay up late to perch on the front steps and rhapsodize over the falling stars.

When two of my husband's co-workers discovered our plans they presented him with a brown paper bag with some "medicine" inside to be taken when things get a little tough.

We had almost a quarter of a mile of our 500 mile trip under our belt when I first expressed a need for first aid, but my husband said to look for the humor in the situation.

Our son, not yet two, had mastered his longest sentence. "I was here first" (actually, it came out *ah fir*). He and his sister, 4, fought for the standing space on the rear center hump which completely obscured their father's rear vision. (*This before the advent of seat belts*).

Eight hours, 50 battles and 25 rest stops later, we pulled into the driveway of our housekeeping rental in Wells Beach, Maine. Once inside, our youngest immediately spilled his drink of water and broke the glass in front of our host.

By week's end our son's total included two shades ripped from their rollers, one bed slightly dampened, one bottle of facial moisturizer dumped on our collection of sea shells and one flooded bathroom.

"See," my husband and I said to each other proudly. "He can be a good boy when he wants to be."

His sister, fastidious and ladylike, browsed with ardor and appreciation in the teeming shops that fill every picturesque coastal village.

"Oh, Daddy, " she exclaimed for all to hear, "see the pretty dish with the bare lady on it."

Determined I should not cook all week long in the cottage's miniature kitchen, my husband took us one evening to a restaurant carpeted in red plush with crystal chandeliers and white tablecloths.

Our daughter, a restaurant goer from six months, primly placed her crimson napkin in her lap, and, lapsing just a little, used her teaspoon to get a sip from her water goblet.

Not to be outdone, her brother neatly placed his napkin over the lighted hurricane lamp and stuck his knife, fork and spoon in his goblet.

It may not sound like progress, but it was a decided improvement over last year when he patted the waitress' posterior every time she leaned over to serve the adjoining table.

(7/69)

Some Lessons Learned Along the Way

1. Never give a child a choice. The question, "Strawberry or vanilla?" can only lead to trouble.

2. A child crying at the top of her lungs can sometimes be stopped if you register amazement at her range and urge her to try for even louder.

3. Never wash a sleepy child's face before putting her to bed. It's easier to launder the pillowcase than put up with a greatly refreshed youngster.

4. Forget a toddler's shoes when he's playing outside in summer. If he's barefoot, you should be able to run almost as fast as he does.

5. Never hang more than one ironed dress at a time in your child's closet. From age 3 on, she'll change outfits every half hour if they're available.

6. It may be advisable to teach your toddler the correct anatomical terms, but you'll be embarrassed less often in public if you stick to cryptic labels known only to the family.

7. Never forget that growing up with television has given your youngsters tactical advantages you can never hope to equal by simply reading.

8. Try not to get involved in spats between your kids and their friends. There never was a childish battle that could equal the furor created by two intelligent, sensible, well-meaning mothers.

9. Avoid letting your toddler see you use an old toothbrush to clean crevices in tile or woodwork. It's not so bad when you catch him in the act, it's when you don't that you can literally grit your teeth.

10. If your children watch you and your husband having a fight, be sure to let them see you make up. It sounds better when they give a blow-by-blow account to the neighbors.

11. Never discuss a relative

unless you can say something nice about him. Guess who will show up next week and guess whose child will remember to ask him about his dilettante ways.

12. Never tell your little genius that he takes after you. He'll turn right around and tie his shoe laces together, spill his milk on his father's trousers or swallow the Indian head penny that rounded out your collection.

(c. 1970)

His Gift to Art –
He Stopped Painting

There is something about fall weather that brings out the art appreciation in our family.

In the last month we've visited five art shows including one staged in a barnyard. If that sounds like a real low, we also hit a high, spending one of those afternoons at the Metropolitan Museum of Art in NYC.

After visiting one of the clothesline shows where pop art was having a field day, my husband eyed an exhibit of bathroom tank floats welded into copper mobiles and announced his intention of entering that particular show next year.

One of the few times he has been stuck by the Muse was shortly before we were married. Using a photograph of me he painted a portrait as a surprise.

His friend Ed advised him that if he wanted the planned wedding to take place, he'd better not show me the finished product.

There was, the friend said, the chance I might interpret the dark, stark rendering as adverse subliminal feelings.

After we were married, he, in the reverse order of most artists who start out trying something simple and gradually arriving at the point where they feel they can tackle a portrait, took to painting colorful vinegar jugs and pots of ivy. His next period (comprising one picture) centered around an ornate Mexican cathedral painted from a picture he'd take years before when stationed at Ft. Bliss, Texas, a short distance from the border.

And with that, he took down his easel and bid the Muse goodbye.

"So, what are you going to enter in the clothesline show?' I wanted to know.

"Next time I go to the

drugstore I'm buying a whole card of nail clippers," was the response.

Something of an artist myself, I had once taken a course at a local art institute with a fellow reporter. Every Monday (our day off at the newspaper) we painted all day long in a third floor studio where July heat boosted the temperature past 90 degrees.

My contribution to the fine arts was a huge canvas on which I splashed an orange guitar, several bilious looking grapefruit and a wine bottle with a very realistic looking label. When someone ventured the opinion that my style was primitive, I took umbrage. Even worse, when the teacher said I needed to learn about values, I was offended, unaware it had something to do with variations in hue intensity. Since then, like my husband, I've been content to indulge my artistic feelings by taking pleasure in others' work.

Johanna, 4, is beginning to show the same appreciation. The guards at the Met agreed you couldn't start your kids too young on the culture kick, but asked that she and her Cousin Annie, 5, refrain from pulling the horse's tail in the medieval armor room.

(c. 1970)

No Milk Cartons On the Table

My husband came home from the library the other night with a book about elegant table settings for me. He does this sort of thing whenever he can't find the kind of historical novel I like.

Sometimes it will be a volume on beautiful homes in America or maybe European antiques. I get a lot of pleasure out of living graciously—if vicariously.

Two of the most interesting books in this category were written by Dorothy Rodgers, wife of composer Richard Rodgers, a student of interior design, a lady of grace, culture and obviously some wealth.

In her first book, "My Favorite Things," she spoke of entertaining weekend guests at their country estate in Connecticut and revealed a custom I rate as the ultimate in luxury:

Every houseguest received a Sunday breakfast tray with their own copy of the Sunday New York Times.

Heaven forbid, wrote the author, that a guest should take his turn at the Sunday paper and find the crossword puzzle already worked.

Mrs. Rodgers had other tips on how to entertain graciously, some of which my husband took to heart.

He was home with the flu for a couple of days and ensconced comfortably on the couch before the television with a pile of books on his stomach. Somehow he managed to work his way through the pile to the bottom.

"You're not serving broccoli tonight for dinner are you, dear?" he called to me. At our house unless we are going out or are having people in, we call the evening meal supper. His use of the word dinner should have tipped me off, but I bit any way.

"Why do you want to know?" I demanded. Mrs. Rodgers, he reminded me, never serves broccoli—because of the strong odor while it is cooking.

"We're not having it for supper, but if we were I'd turn on the fan," I shot back and returned to the kitchen.

Two seconds later he was calling again, this time to make sure I was toasting the white bread.

"Toasting the white bread?" I echoed stupidly. Mrs. Rodgers, I was informed, declares that no white bread ever makes its way to her table without being toasted.

Since then I have taken the trouble to keep all the gracious living tomes apart from his piles of mystery collections.

I do make a point of keeping the milk cartons off the supper table. And there's a table cloth on the kitchen table after I discovered it wipes up cleaner than the formica top which is inclined to streak. But it's plastic.

Probably the ultimate blunder against true elegance is that we almost always eat in the kitchen. The dining room bluish green rug hides chocolate cake crumbs, grape jelly and even stomped on peas. But not even it would take kindly to the nightly occurrence of spilled milk.

(c. 1970)

Giving A Party

Jean Kerr is a writer and party giver after my own heart. In her latest book, "Penny Candy", she explained how she went about entertaining.

After some vacillating, she would call up a friend, utter an expletive and announce in mournful tones that she was giving a party, and did they want to come.

I empathize. It's not that I don't like having people about. I do. And it's not the problem of what to serve. I learned in my college days you can serve pig knuckles and lentil soup to absolutely anybody and get away with it—if you've got enough nerve. And I do.

My problem is as a disorganized housekeeper without parallel it's a matter of getting the house ready.

I know there are women who keep house in such a manner that their husbands could call 10 minutes past midnight and say they're bringing 18 people home for a midnight snack.

In less than 8 minutes these paragons are out of bed, dressed in casual chic, fashion wig on and cheese fondue thawing on the back burner. Maybe, just maybe, they might have to refold the evening paper in the family room should anyone wander in there.

There are others, of course who, although excellent managers, refuse to allow any kind of gathering in their homes without at least three weeks notice. That's how long it takes to do the equivalent of both spring and winter housecleaning in an already impeccable dwelling.

They need to clean the attic, straighten the kids' junk drawers and sterilize the laundry tubs in the basement. It also helps their mental state if they can get their husbands to take the car in for a fresh lube job.

My own strategy is somewhat different: I consider it important when giving a dinner party to make sure all the dining room chairs are both empty of model cars and dry to the touch. (The baby does tend to climb on them minus diaper. I also check to see if the missing basket of ironing might be under the table.)

Next firmly bolt and lock the family bathroom and clean the powder room, making sure to remove rubber ducky from the sink, Sunday's book review magazine and six plastic aerosol can tops.

Vacuum living room couch crevices. A visiting priest once plunged his hand down between cushions and came up with a mummified hot dog, three M&Ms and a sparkler from a recent Fourth of July celebration.

Place throw rug over spot in front of green chair, draw curtains to hide streaked windows and remove baby from top of dining room table. Answer doorbell, hug guests, forget house.

(c. 1971)

Easter's Meaning

I do not know how parents who disdain the idea of a life hereafter explain death to their children. It is hard enough even when you trust that dying is but a rebirth.

On Friday the five-year-old who has been discussing cemeteries with her best friend got to the nitty gritty.

But if we go to heaven why do we have to go into the ground?" Cara wanted to know.

It was bedtime and conversation then is usually a stalling technique. But the answer to this question wouldn't wait.

"The important part of us goes to heaven. We don't need our bodies," I reassured her.

She was adamant. "Well, I want mine!"

"God promised us our bodies and souls would all go back together later."

She, who has trouble differentiating between two days and a week, wanted an exact time. "When? Two years, three years, when?"

I was losing control of the conversation. I told her the truth as I understand it. "Jesus said if we loved Him and trusted Him we don't ever have to be afraid."

As she chewed on that, I tried a diversionary tactic not immediately aware of the irony. "Think of something pleasant. Think about Easter." She settled down, her Easter a montage of a trip to her grandparents, a candy-filled basket and a new, long, yellow dress.

On Saturday night we went to Mass fulfilling our obligation for what used to be known as Passion Sunday. I listened to the miracle of the sermon, Jesus raising Lazarus from the dead. A new peace settled on me and I looked over at Cara, but the afternoon of hard swimming had taken its toll and she was asleep on her father's shoulder.

On Sunday we were out of the house and on our way to the Montezuma Swamps by 9 a.m.

Just inside the entrance to the wild life refuge, we spotted three deer and when the kids went to the chain fence the deer came bounding from the thicket to munch the heavily salted pretzel that was offered.

Farther down the trail we watched the brilliant blue of the sky turn almost black as wave upon wave of geese headed for the marsh.

On our left, the tall winter wheat they would feed on waved in the slight breeze. On our right, the huge carp could be sighted in the icy water. Then a helicopter swooped low and a "zillion" geese took to the air in a frenzy of swooping wings and flashing white underbodies.

Winter weary, I took in the warmth of the sun, the melting and mixing of snow and mud and the honks of the geese.

I thought of spring and new beginnings and Jesus raising Lazarus from the grave. A promise worth waiting for. A promise to trust in. I looked for the five-year-old to pass on new reassurance. But she was hunting snails in the mud and snow.

(c. 1974)

Why Parenthood?

During a recent TV program several couples explained why they preferred to remain childless.

Some cited ecological reasons, others mentioned nomadic life styles and some pointed out that their personal goals and children simply could not mesh.

One couple was more to the point and possibly more honest than the others. Raising children was something they did not want to be bothered with. Yes, they said, you could call it pure selfishness.

The label I'd bestow? Immature. Not selfish.

I, the mother of three, am the selfish one, greedy for all the extra dimensions that raising children add to one's life.

First, there was the anticipation as we waited for each of ours to arrive. Then there were the sublime moments as we caught sight of each for the very first time.

I think of the softness, the warmth, the feel of them in my arms, body against body.

I think of that first moment when they recognized me as not just another pair of arms to rescue them from the crib, to hold the bottle.

I think of the first step walking between the outstretched arms of their father and me. I think of the moist kisses, swift hugs, and soft voices learning to say "I love you" back.

The messy times, and there are plenty, are somehow diminished by time and our growth as a family.

A couple of years ago in despair over the serious illness of my much-loved mother-in-law, I remember reaching blindly for our toddler son and holding him quietly in my arms. Such comfort radiated from that small body I can feel it still.

Yesterday the four-year-old learned to jump rope. Today she learned to tie her shoes. I cannot even for a second try to explain her joy or what I felt watching her self pride.

When the six-year-old comes

in wonderfully dirty from sliding down a mud mountain and tells me he doesn't need a bath because he had one the night before I gurgle inside over his gorgeous logic.

And when our nine-year-old from time to time reveals brief moments of insight into the adult world, I am agog with the wonder of this new person emerging from the child.

Some days the burdens of parenthood are overwhelming. I know of no mother or father who would deny this. There are times when I think I'm managing a circus instead of rearing three kids. They embarrass us, anger us, frustrate us and even while they are encouraging our candidacies for a mental institution, the splendor of their light never dims.

(c. 1973)

Call Me A Sticky Bun

If it is true that you are what you eat then I am a panful of homemade sticky pecan rolls, a six-egg chocolate layer cake and a quadruple portion of my mother's potato salad.

With the help of an expert specializing in obesity, who approaches the problem from a psychological standpoint, I have discovered a few things about myself.

To wit: I eat when I am bored, when I am uptight, when I am happy, when I am sad, when I am in need of a friend, when I am surrounded by friends, when I have something to celebrate, when I have nothing to celebrate, when everybody else is eating, when nobody else is eating, when food is highly visible, when food is nowhere in sight etc. etc. etc..

"Obviously," concluded the psychologist, only somewhat wryly, "food is very important to you."

Ah, if he only knew. I have tried to explain how intertwined are the good times of my childhood with a table laden to excess.

I doubt it is possible to explain this to anyone (a) Whose grandparents didn't emigrate here in the early part of this century from a European country where having a meal of bread twice a day was considered a triumph; (b) Who didn't have a mother and two grandmothers, to say nothing of aunts, all dedicated to the art of cooking varied and substantial meals based on both the Old World and new American cuisines; (c) Who didn't begin life in the middle of the Great Depression.

I have tried explaining this to the psychologist who remains completely unimpressed. Aware of the folly of taking something away without replacing it with something else, he has offered me the principle of substitution.

On the theory that a body in motion finds the chewing and swallowing processes hampered, he has recommended exercise. I can now jump rope with both feet off the ground. I jog. I run up and down the cellar steps as if the devil were hiding in the crawl space just waiting to jump out at me. And I can walk—for hours.

Thus far, if put to a comparison test, the six-egg layer cake would win hands down. But, who knows—that may not always be the case. Outrunning your own three panting kids is the kind of thrill the Betty Crocker people haven't yet thought of packaging.

(c. 1974)

Delighting in the Fury

This morning our backyard, the small woods and the field beyond it are icily majestic. Yesterday I sat for part of the afternoon gazing out the glass door at the storm, delighting in its fury.

Yesterday's vehement winds, whipping and bending the dogwood and the willows and some of the little white pines, made me fear for the trees, but brought the same kind of pleasure I remember from the summer thunder storms of my childhood.

Obviously I have been fortunate enough not to have experienced a natural disaster and the prospect of a hurricane or tornado invokes the same negative feelings in me as in everyone else.

But there was little to fear in the intensity of those long ago frenzied rains. My maternal grandparents lived in the country. The house, woodshed and springhouse along with the chicken coop and outhouse backed up against a mountain.

A stream marked the opposite boundary.

The one-room schoolhouse my mom and her siblings attended, the general store and five or six houses stood on the other side of the stream and wooden bridge. Our isolation was complete except for Gilbert, the Indian who lived in a shack high on the mountain behind us. And he visited infrequently.

The front porch, only 10 yards or so from the stream, held a long greenish-blue bench, a railroad station cast-off, and a high back swing which Grandpa had hung from the porch rafters.

When the rain began and we were called from the banks of the "crick" where we made lovely, if fragile, clay bowls, Louise, my same age aunt, and I would scurry to the shelter of the porch.

Louise would then sneak upstairs and grab a quilt from our bed and she and I would huddle under it on the swing and watch the lightning explode over the bridge.

Each thunderous clap would send us diving under the quilt until the steamy closeness would force us up for air.

No need to worry about the electricity or the phone being knocked out. There was neither. Fire would have been a different matter as there was no squad, volunteer or otherwise.

But we were oblivious to the potential for destruction anyway. Only the power, the force and the ragged, jagged beauty of it all had our attention. Fear mixed with fascination kept us a captive audience. At night my cowardly streak would take over and I would quake in bed at the sound of the rushing creek and the mournful cry of the whippoorwill, remembering all too vividly the story somebody told about spotting a bobcat in one of the nearby hollows.

But in a daylight storm with my intrepid barefoot aunt at my side and a patchwork quilt as our shield we were invincible.

(c. 1974)

Seed Package Poetry

One of the pluses of raising children is that in their first few years, at least, we are sometimes privy to their inner thoughts, to the turnings of the mental process.

Before they master the succinct phrase, the ambiguous shrug, the duplicitous rejoinder, they tell it like it is. Sometimes it comes out pure poetry.

Not too long ago our youngest and her father were having a quiet talk, the five-year-old on his lap.

"Tell me," I heard him question her at one point, "What do you dream about when you go to sleep?"

"Oh," she said quickly without a pause, "things in barns."

Strange, I thought, my own mental image of things in barns predisposed toward tractors and hay rakes and other mundane implements.

"Things in barns?" echoed her father puzzled. (He later confessed he'd been conjuring up pictures of shovels and other tools himself.)

"Oh," she said softly, her brown eyes growing darker and larger by the second, "Things like little lambs."

"Ah," said her father enchanted with the answer, "and when you are not dreaming of little lambs, what then?"

Again quickly, "Well, then I dream of tulips in the grass and frogs in winter." She'd been dipping into Walt Whitman obviously.

A week or so later she was watching "Little House on the Prairie" with her older brother and sister when a scene of a pioneer woman in labor suddenly riveted everybody's attention until the cry of an infant signaled the birth.

She turned to me and asked for the umpteenth time (her best friend Jenna has a new baby brother) "Now, how is it that the baby gets inside the mother?"

Trying to gauge just how much information she would want this time, I began my usual preliminary.

"Well, you know," I began,

"the father gives the mother a seed..."

"Oh yes," she interrupted excitedly, thinking just one step ahead of her words, "and the seed packages have pictures of babies on them, right?"

In her concentration she didn't see the eyes of those around her soften and mouths crinkle at the imagery she had evoked. No idea she had just composed a poem.

(c. 1974)

Happy Birthday, Jo

Our oldest complains that while I frequently write about her younger brother and sister, she is given short shrift. I remind her that when she was young (and anecdote material) I wrote about her often. She reminds me that she could not read then and I have not bothered to save what I wrote. This then is a letter to her on the occasion of a birthday.

Dearest Jo: Somebody has said that the tenth birthday is a milestone in a child's life. Well, maybe. But I find that the milestones, as I see them, have nothing to do with calendars or numbers.

I am delighted and only the tiniest bit sad that you are ten. On your fifth birthday I wept a few tears. Your father chided me for imagining you already grown up and gone away from us. He said I was silly but I forgave him because inside he is, I know, even more sentimental about his children than I.

I love having you ten. Not only have you since mastered those nuisance chores such as tying your own shoe laces, getting in and out of snow clothes and washing your hair, but you can scramble better eggs than I can. You also can interpret printed instructions which I find impossible and size up an emotion-laden situation with finesse whether it be your father and I having words, a joust with a sales clerk or two of your girlfriends in a snit.

But best of all I like having you ten because now we can and do communicate with language as well as hugs and squeezes. Lucid conversation has always been one of my prime treats. Conversing with one's own child is a rare pleasure, worth cultivating and worth waiting for.

At the beginning of this letter I talked about milestones. I remember bringing you home from the hospital. Your father and I had been married for a little more than a year. I remember looking at the two of you together in our own home and thinking that never before had I felt so much concentrated love.

Dad walked around with you in his arms that night, upstairs and down, showing you each room, explaining every detail to you as if you were a much desired, prospective tenant whom he was trying to persuade to stay.

Nothing you did was insignificant to us. We did not wear our hearts on our sleeves. We pasted them on our foreheads above prideful, doting smiles.

Your great-grandmother, Annie, when she learned of your brother's imminent arrival, said she was surprised. She thought we would not want to share our love for you with another.

But it was precisely because we loved you so much that we wanted to increase the circle...

And because we loved John so much, Cara was added to the fold.

In this day and age of women's lib and Zero Population Growth,

it is not very popular to talk of enjoying your children or extolling the advantages of parenthood.

I know I can speak for your father as well as myself in saying that whatever else we do with our lives, it must necessarily pale in the challenge and accomplishments of rearing you all to be loving, responsible adults.

This is not to say it has been effortless. Bringing up kids is not easy. There you are, one moment a kind, well-behaved, lovely and intelligent human being. The next I find I am mother to a karate-chopping, ten-year-old nitpicking cowboy.

The other day you surprised me by throwing your arms around my neck and whispering, "I love you." That kind of spontaneous expression becomes more rare with each year you accumulate—and more precious, as you yourself are.

Happy birthday, Sweetheart.
(1975)

Advice from a Novelist

In an interview-award wining novelist Joyce Carol Oates said that the reason she was able to accomplish so much (she teaches also) was that she had at one point made up her mind not to do anything she didn't want to. I, for one, think her philosophy is fantastic. And so tomorrow I will not:

Make the coffee, reconstitute the juice, pour out the cereal; run the four daily loads through the washer, fold the contents of the dryer, put clothes away; load the dishwasher, clear the table, sweep the floor; put the family room back together, take out the newspapers; wash the two living room windows, rehang the drapes back from the cleaners; hunt for the missing library books, return the playground chairman's call; mail our incipient kindergartner's health form, make one peanut butter and jelly sandwich for her lunch, wipe out the refrigerator when she spills her juice, sweep up the floor where most of her lunch ends up; make the beds, dust the furniture, run the vacuum cleaner; go to the store for bread and milk, plan and cook dinner, reload the dishwasher after the kids' initial try; weed around the tomato plants; get the slugs out of the strawberry patch; dig holes for the two small pin oaks I bought at the half price sale; start packing the camping gear, bake a triple batch of chocolate chip cookies to take with us, call various stores to locate luggage rack ropes; cut off the seven-year-old's jeans for shorts; hem the 10-year-old's new skooter skirt; take in three sizes the father's day T-shirt I made; and finally I will not repaint the laundry room with the semi gloss lemon ice I bought two weeks ago; clean behind the washer where the dryer lint vented nor try to capture the horse fly that zoomed in when I was trying to let the steam out.

The day after tomorrow, however, I expect to get up very very early. I have the feeling it will be an extremely busy day.

Honorable Mention?

In his *Impressions of America*, Oscar Wilde wrote: *"Over the piano was printed a notice. Please do not shoot the pianist. He is doing his best."*

I'm thinking of hanging the same sign in the kitchen or maybe the front hall. Mine, of course, will say homemaker. I do not play the piano.

It will replace the "Honorable Mention" placard which the children's father brought home after our eldest evaluated one of my gourmet meals thusly.

In keeping with the spirit of the situation, I taped my "award" on the hood over the kitchen stove, where it stood as kind of judgment on all my culinary efforts, until the steam from countless pots of pasta took its toll. The Scotch tape lost its glue and the sign fell—probably into a batch of fettuccini.

Actually I'm sort of sorry about the sign's starchy demise. I liked it. In its own way it reflected something very basic about me.

The truth is that I am more than satisfied having achieved mere adequacy as a cook. Ditto for my housekeeping ability, which after 11 years of trying, is still somewhat below par.

In the scheme of things I have come to regard those so-called womanly talents relatively unimportant, implicit in the marriage vows maybe, but hardly of staggering consequence.

I know a lot of women will disagree with me, believing that the best way to show one's familial devotion is through the compilation of a six-layer Viennese Torte, a bottom sheet that is tucked in evenly all way around and home-made sweaters for one and all. I say "de gustibus non est disputandum."

No, if ever I am to rise beyond the honorable category, aspiring to the glorious prize ribbon divisions, let me labor and grow in an area whose rewards are less transient that a perfect chocolate soufflé.

I can see it all now. Blue

ribbons for applying just the right pressure in kissing scraped knees. A red ribbon for ignoring months on end the dripping faucet in the powder room. A white ribbon (third prize but still in the winner's circle) for subbing at home plate when the catcher is called home for supper.

And maybe the ultimate accolade: A standing ovation from my crew when I manage to sit through a whole showing of Frankenstein and/or a Disney movie.

(c. 1975)

Don't Choose Me, Lord

My thoughts returned recently to my freshman year at Villa Maria, a small college for women in Erie. (*Villa Maria* has since merged with *Gannon College*). Most of the students were day students. Only 14 of us freshmen were boarders, a hallway separating the school wing from the convent.

I don't know if the proximity was responsible, but during the spring of the first and only year I was to spend there, a total of six friends crept, one by one, into my room to confide that they had come to a momentous decision.

By the time the fourth one put in an appearance, she didn't have to finish the sentence. I would do it for her. "You are going to join the sisters at the convent," I would say, and she would nod happily.

We would hug each other. I would offer congratulations, and she would go off down the hall to confide in still another, while I would sit on my bed with my head in my hands.

Secretly I was horrified. In spite of a Catholic upbringing, which included being versed in the ardor of the saints, I was at least 20 years away from knowing about the kind of love that out burns any worldly relations.

More importantly, at least from my point of view, there was a new baby at home. My sister Judy was born August 23, just before I left for college. Her arrival 12 years after the birth of brother Sam , had taken us all by surprise. Pink and beautiful, this new sister was deliciously soft and huggable. At 18 I was not much taken with the idea of marriage, but I was definitely enthralled by babies and hoped they belonged in my future.

"Don't choose me, Lord," I prayed guiltily that spring and it was with great relief I left that convent-college atmosphere in June, convinced He hadn't.

But of course he had. Although for something different. Obviously the Lord didn't think I was any more fit to be a nun than I did. Argumentative, independent, stubborn and mostly mouth, I wasn't fit for anything much, except to be left alone to grow up.

Well, I wasn't left alone. But I was helped to grow up—slowly. And somewhere in the middle of it all I was able to see that in spite of my independent self, it was not I who was calling the shots. The choice of what I should do with my life had been made for me, long before I ever couched that fearful prayer.

As Mother's Day approaches I think of that long ago plea and the Lord's almost certain amusement as I go about my day, tearing out my hair, screaming sometimes at the top of my lungs, and wondering aloud what I ever did to deserve such an incorrigible crew.

And I imagine His smile last thing at night as I thank Him for my vocation, and assure Him that all these years later, I'm still enthralled by babies—both the little kind and those asleep down the hall—now grown up.

(c. 1976)

Dangly Earrings Plus a 'Fuzzy'

As birthdays go, it was a super one. Gifts, cards and long distance calls made the day a memorable one. Among the kids' gifts was a spider plant from our son, purchased at a barn sale, a decorated tin box to add to my collection from our older daughter, and a packet from their younger sister swathed in tissue and yards of Scotch tape.

Inside was a dangly pair of delicate earrings and a tanned rabbit skin.

I oohed and aahed and learned the gifts were part of an exchange she had made with the first grader across the aisle at school. She had traded pencils for the loot.

Because I've given away junk jewelry to the kids, the exchange seemed harmless enough. Closer scrutiny, however, showed the earrings to be better quality than anything I'd ever disposed of. I sent her back to school with

them the next morning to give to her friend.

She returned with them that afternoon, again wrapped and taped and ready for presentation. It was okay with the friend's mother, she explained.

I wore the dangly earrings to Friendly's the next night after futile explanations that they didn't go with my usual rustic attire. The gift-giver beamed throughout the meal.

Back home I put the earrings away for safekeeping, and began searching for her friend's name and a telephone number. No luck in discerning the right spelling. I tossed the scrap of rabbit skin on the closet shelf and forgot about both for several weeks until a recent conference night. Explaining the situation to the first grade teacher, I was given the family's phone number.

I called the next day. "Oh, dear, oh, dear," was the response.

"Do they look like looped silver thread?" the little friend's mother asked softly. I said that they did. She said she had a pin that matched and that the set was real silver. No, she did not know they were missing.

There was still the matter of the rabbit skin. "Rabbit skin? Rabbit skin?" she puzzled. "Oh, no! It's her brother's *fuzzy*," said the trader's mother.

Restoration was made later in the day with me apologizing for taking so long to call her and she for not being aware of the initial transaction.

Back home I expounded on the wisdom of limiting trades to paper dolls etc. And I reassured the youngest, it really is the thought behind the gift that counts.

(c. 1976)

The Dog Lover

I did not intend to love our little dog as I have come to do.

She was to be the children's pet, tolerated for their sake. We would put up with her as best we could.

A mixture of water spaniel and cocker spaniel, she was purchased for a nominal fee as gift for the youngest's birthday against our better judgment. We had been saying, "No" for nearly 12 years to the pleas for an animal, any animal.

Animals, we told our crew repeatedly, were dirty, pesky and an inconvenience. From time to time, we allowed goldfish or an occasional turtle in the house and once we let the oldest bring home a pair of gerbils from the classroom for a weekend visit.

We smirked at those pet owners who couldn't seem to distinguish between pets and children and we worried over reports that some pets ate better than many people.

We were repelled (and continue to be) by most of the pet food TV commercials which pander to people with more sentimentality than sense.

We finally gave in to the idea of a pet when Cara, 7, began bringing in wandering mutts and crying conspicuously, if silently, when they would wander off again.

The night we brought the pup home, she fit in both my hands. Her tiny heart leaped violently in fear of our strangeness and the absence of her mother and siblings. She cried that night and several thereafter. Instead of anger and annoyance, something else took hold and grew inside this "grandmother" as I was designated by the mother-owner.

Perhaps it has something to do with maternal instinct. We are used to responding to tiny, helpless creatures that require love and attention to survive.

Whatever the reason, I appear to be smitten. I feel pride when she responds to a command, a sense of wonder to see the graceful black body dance in enjoyment over being outdoors and definite tenderness as she greets us wildly after an hour's separation.

A burden as I feared? Of course. But a small price to pay for the love she lavishes on us and the enjoyment she brings.

(c. 1976)

Smart As A...Mutt

There are three, maybe four, kinds of people on this earth. They can be categorized thusly:

1. dog lovers
2. dog haters
3. Those who tolerate dogs, but have no strong feelings one way or the other.

The fourth possible category includes those who are afraid of, or are allergic to dogs, and are too intimidated to find out which of the above groups they belong to.

I belong to the first category—except when our mutt, Clementine, turns me into an idiot, which is fairly frequently. A black lab of sorts, she, at 10 months, is charming, willful, undisciplined, lovable and a general pain in the neck (and sometimes even lower regions).

Logically, enough, I guess, she obeys only one person in the house—the master who is very stingy when it comes to bestowing attention and affection upon her.

The kids and I, on the other hand, act complete fools, talking dog talk (akin to baby talk, only worse) scratching her stomach for long periods of time when she so desires, slipping choice morsels to her under the table and putting up with all kinds of outrageous behavior.

The other day at the bank's drive up window, the mutt responded to friendly overtures from the teller with loud barking and dashing about on the station wagon deck.

Embarrassed, I was eager for the business to be transacted so I could disappear. When the window opened, however, it was not an envelope. Instead two dog biscuits lay there, signaling, I guess, I'm not the first to go banking with a mutt.

My worst problem is how to retrieve Clem when she escapes out the front door as the kids are leaving for the bus. She did this recently in pouring rain. Still in housecoat, I cajoled, pleaded, and begged her to return. No luck. Worried about the imminent arrival of the bus, I tried a fool proof method.

Still in housecoat, I dashed out into the rain and opened the car door and in my most beguiling voice trilled, "Wanna go for a ride?"

She ran up, surveyed me critically, her tongue hanging out, one ear rakishly askew, and backed off.

Was this creature really smart enough to know I didn't go out in the car in a housecoat? No.

Then a light dawned and I went back inside and flung my purse over my robed shoulder, keys in hand. This time I jingled the keys, and after a quick glance at my "business" outfit of bathrobe cum purse, Clem hopped in.

Jubilant, though drenched, I warned the still waiting kids not to tell their father of the incident, led the dog back in to the house, and hoped none of the neighbors had been watching.

(c. 1976)

Learning from the Experts

I was one of those obtuse mothers who thought she always knew best. No longer. I have seen the error of my ways.

Take the matter of the cocoa cup and the spoon. For years I've been telling the oldest to remove the spoon from the cup when she sips it.

Not only is it bad manners, I pointed out, but the spoon threatens to poke her eye out each time she raises it.

She listened, did as she was bid—until the next time.

One morning after the crew left for school, I decided to see for myself what was the attraction.

I made a cup of cocoa, stuck a spoon in it and hoisted it. Needless to say I was blown away. The cocoa was far more delicious with the utensil tilting dangerously in the mug. To test further, I took the spoon out and drank. Nowhere near as tasty as the swallow plus spoon.

It was then I vowed to take our kids seriously and learn all I could from them.

From our son I discovered that when one is in a hurry it is far speedier to pull clean socks on over dirty ones (no doubt, worn to bed) than changing them.

From the youngest, I learned that combining something you love doing with something you'd rather not, makes the time go faster. To wit: Practicing disco steps and violin at the same time.

This same child also taught me something about gustatory pleasures, e.g., mashed potato sandwiches, peanut butter on potato chips and green beans doused in catsup.

As for the 13-year-old, she has done much to revolutionize my housekeeping. Some of her more daring and innovative concepts concern:

A. The mail. (When in doubt,

throw it out.)

B. The laundry (Dark and whites washed together produce gray—an acceptable neutral.)

C. Cooking. (If God had not wanted us to rely on cans, He wouldn't have invented them.)

(c. 1977)

Grim News

After giving the rice a stir, I spread the evening paper out. The news is grim. Planned Parenthood will spend $1 million to convince the country that abortion is right and good. They have hired a public relations firm to spread the message. It appears, however, that their fight is more against antiabortion forces than it actually is pro women. Reading between the lines, one learns that the antis have been too successful and must be counteracted. Women must be told they have a choice.

From upstairs the strains of "Carnival of Venice" come drifting down with only one or two false notes. Not bad for a beginning trumpet player. I think about the "choices" made affecting our family.

I read on and the face of a friend comes to mind. For all of the seven years I have known her, she has wanted a baby desperately, a baby of her own. She has a baby, at long last, a baby of her own—although another woman has given it birth. The radiance on my friend's beautiful freckled face these days is blinding.

The trumpet player comes downstairs to raid the refrigerator. Too near suppertime. I interfere and we have words. We are more often at odds with each other than not, but it is a surface thing. Underneath, fierce emotion binds us. He was introduced to us (his father, older sister and me) when he was five months. He said, "Ah-Bah," and we fell in love.

His younger sister comes in and turns on the TV and a smile plays across her face as some inanity takes place on the screen. At nine years, she knows more about the joy of living and loving, and how to communicate it to others than do some adults who have lived ten times as long.

She knows, for example, that contrary to popular belief, life sometimes IS a musical comedy; that money is best spent on presents for others and that every unfamiliar face is a potential friend. She was three months when she first lit up our lives.

From the living room comes the lilting sounds of Beethoven's "Fur Elise" as the oldest readies for a piano lesson. But for the "choices" made by two other women, she might have been an only child, a fate some say is not so bad, but she would not agree.

I go back to the newspaper and read on and mourn for all those lives that will have no "choices". I think about the slogans that will be written by the most clever, most persuasive of copy writers, whose glib words sell soap and cars today, and tomorrow will doom babies. I wonder if any of them will care or is it just another job.

(c. 1978)

...And He Must Like Dogs

Our older daughter and I are having a conversation about men at the supper table. It is in jest of course—she's only 14—but as often is the case in this kind of bantering, there is a serious vein running underneath.

When it comes time to pick a husband (15 years hence I think optimistically) she must look for certain characteristics.

He must be good (morally sound) and kind, intelligent and have a strong sense of humor. Absence of any one of those virtues is a serious defect. "And, of course, he must like dogs," I conclude. The other four at the table give me one of those looks which mean "she's gone off the deep end again" and resume eating their beans and hotdogs.

The last is not a requisite for all women, only for those who like dogs. And she does.

Thus, if she can find a mate who feels the same it will save her

a lot of grief. I should know.

Some of her father's and my very best fights have been over our dog Clementine.

He takes umbrage over the fact that every morning at 6, when the paperboy opens the storm door to put the paper inside, the dog goes into hysterics. The master thinks that after two years the animal should know that the kid is friend, not foe.

He also takes issue with floating dog hairs, window sills pawed to the bare wood (Clem likes looking out the window), and that she doesn't like to eat her supper until we start ours.

In retaliation he calls Clem who is definitely a she, IT.

In recent months he appears to have mellowed somewhat and there is the increasing possibility that he is not as averse to this particular mutt as he sometimes make out.

The dog meets him at the

door with the same unalloyed joy whether he has been gone for half an hour or two weeks, indicating, perhaps, that behind our backs he has given her some cause for such devotion.

(c. 1979)

Green Pastures

The creek (pronounced crick) is high and I think about cautioning our two younger children to watch their step, but then think better of it. There is a sandy mud bar directly ahead.

With their grandfather, they are baiting a hook and preparing to cast their line into the "honey of a hole" under the bent willow tree. Trouble is, there is only one pole for two kids, and the fireworks are bound to start soon.

The oldest and I walk away, charmed as always by the fast moving stream which forms the curving northern boundary of nearly 40 acres of pasture, woodland and swamp.

It is our first trip to camp since last fall, and while there is not a time when it is not beautiful, its special quality early in May is not to be matched.

The trees are all in bud, some of the earliest already decked out in pale green lacy foliage. Underfoot in the shuffle of last year's leaves, moss-covered fallen trees and underbrush, the wildflowers are putting on their first splendiferous show.

Here and there are purple (or is it mauve?) hepatica, little white blooms, which we know as May flowers, and then some showier yellow spikes called dog's tooth violet or trout lily.

The dog is, as usual, in a state of wild ecstasy, free of fetters.

As we walk along the bank, upstream from the fishermen, Clementine is in and out of the water, pounding through the mud, whipping through the swampy murk. She jumps all over us to make sure we know how much she is enjoying herself.

A tinier stream crisscrosses the land between the camp and the moving boundary, and my dad has fashioned wooden bridges across the water.

We bound across them now to climb the bank to the camp and check on supper time. My mom is in the big room that serves as living room, kitchen, dining room and overflow sleeping quarters.

She has not joined us in our walks. Communing with nature for her means hitting the golf course.

Mom is playing solitaire, one eye on the chicken and sauce on the back of the stove. My brother, who is joining us for supper, will arrive in half an hour she says. I head up the old railroad grade, part of the old Shawmut line.

More swamp on the right filled with marsh marigold, butter yellow petals against the heart-shaped green leaves. The dog runs ahead on the abandoned railroad bed known variously as the Appian Way and Daisy Lane. I bend down and find a rusted spike, the tracks ripped out long ago.

All around, gray birch, gnarled apple trees, hemlock and poplar intermingle with the greenish yellow of new honeysuckle and burgeoning blackberry bramble. I wish again for the gift of poetry. Nothing less will do for the beauty, the peace, the miracle of spring's rebirth.

After supper we take the same walk. All too soon it is dusk and it's time to start loading kids, dog and fishing pole into Dad's Blazer. From the swamp comes the shrilling of the spring peepers. Oh, to pack it all up and take it home.

(c. 1979)

Camp Costa

Two of my nephews and I have gone to camp. With 17 of us in one house, large though it may be, the mood turns frantic very early in the day.

My sisters and I have converged upon our parents, and since the ménage includes five teenagers, a vacation mentality prevails from sunup to sunup. Some of us, it appears, need a respite.

Sam, 9, and Joshua, 6, are going cray fishing. I am going along to supervise, and take in the solitude of the 40 wooded acres.

The woods are dense, cool and fragrant on this 90ish day, the valley floor thick with fern, moss, wintergreen and some tiny flowers I cannot identify. Marvin Creek, known as "the crick," borders the property on the north, hills rising steeply on the opposite side.

The boys wear old sneakers and swim trunks, carry a galvanized pail, and are immediately at home in the shallow, swiftly flowing water.

Clementine, our dog, takes longer to enter the water, preferring instead to chew on sour grass, plow through the mud bar and chase a butterfly.

I wade through the creek to the opposite side, find a fairly wide stone to sit on, and tug on it until I get it to the water's edge. Just then Sam appears with his bucket and pours water all over it.

"There Aunt Trish," he says proudly, "It's clean. Now you can sit on it." It's also wet. I thank him and pull over a thick tree limb and sit down quickly before he can dampen it, and stick my feet in the water.

Clementine wanders past and I murmur a greeting. "Having fun, Superdog?"

Josh hears me and splashes through the water to my side. He looks at Clem and then at me. "My dog Albert can fly," he says.

"No kidding?" Maybe he'll teach Clem how."

He is thoughtful, only a very tiny twinkle in the eye to indicate he is teasing. "No, I think it is something every dog has to teach himself."

"You are probably right," I say and roil the water with a little toe action.

Josh heads back toward the middle of the stream where Sam is having an inordinate amount of luck. He turns before he reaches Sam and yells over to me, "Actually, Albert probably was born knowing how."

An hour later, damp, muddy and pleased with ourselves, we head back to the camp, to build a dam for the crayfish in tiny rivulets closer to the cabin.

"Anybody want a sandwich?"

I ask.

Sam yells up from his dam site. "You go fix them and we'll eat them." It seems a fair enough deal. And I go do as I'm bid.

At some point I follow the boys back to the crick. I sit for a long time on the now dry rock and listen to my nephews' excited chatter as they catch more crayfish. The running creek hidden by tall grasses, reflecting the sun and blue sky above, is balm to the soul. I think of the blessings of family, green hills and meandering streams and of the memories that are being created this day.

(c. 1978)

Lesson In Humility

Being the mother of a teen can be a humbling experience. In a five-minute period the other day, I learned that my lipstick was too red, hair too gray, boots "gross", turtleneck crooked, favorite radio station square, wallpaper choice monotonous, grocery cart items boring, and taste in literature, deplorable. (A woman my age should have progressed past the romantic saga.)

All this was levied in very kind tones, of course, because the almost 15-year-old is very kind to older people, particularly those ancients with whom she shares a house.

Some might take umbrage at such straightforward criticism, but mothers know better. I thanked her for her observations, promised to try harder and in the proper obsequious tone, asked if there was anything else on her mind...

Well, she said, since I asked.... I was far too permissive with her brother and sister and much too strict with her; too many starchy meals had been served in recent days and had I never heard of sirloin; didn't I think her room should be the first done over in a general sprucing up of the house; had I ever thought of hiring a housekeeper (she'd been doing dishes for more than half her life); how did I feel about her flying down to Florida to join her grandparents for a respite? And why is it that I seem to treat the dog better than I treat her?

To the first two items I responded wittily, "Is that so?" the next three earned an unequivocal "NO" and to the last, "Because the dog doesn't give me any lip."

(c. 1980)

Thank God for That Little Bite

Every clan has its own private language replete with sayings they have collected over the years. They don't mean much to anyone outside the group, but to those in the circle the retelling of such anecdotes is integral to a celebratory gathering.

Because holidays have a way of dredging up the past with a vengeance, we've had a lot of these "historical" moments and words replayed recently. Interesting that most of them deal with food in one way or the other.

The first that comes to mind was contributed to our collection by my husband's maternal grandfather, Big Tim Fitzgerald, who at the end of every meal had his own way of remarking on the bounty of the Lord.

"Thank God for that little bite," he would say, no matter how small or big the meal.

Over the years we have utilized that particular phrase many a time, usually, when there have been too many "bites".

Big Tim's daughter, (and my husband's mother) Nell, one of ten children, tips the scale at 88 pounds. It is superfluous to say that eating either during or between meals is not one of her passions.

Yet she has punctuated many a supper by getting up to briskly clear the table and announce, "Well the fun's over for another day."

On my side of the family, Uncle Al would invariably amuse the younger members of the group waiting for the sweet that would finish off the meal by demanding, "What's for berserk?" It took years to come up an equally inane answer. When somebody, knowing there was shortcake waiting in the kitchen, shot back, "Struggleberries" it took and became part of the lexicon.

Grandma Borelli, a woman to delight the heart of every chauvinist, has, as long as I can remember, inquired solicitously of every male around the table, whether it be two or 20 of us:

"Sam, (Bobby, Paul, Ernest, Johnny Boy), she will ask in genuine concern, "Did you make out?"

Since the person in question has already had two helpings of everything, about all he can do is shake his head up and down and try to make it to the living room couch where he will be sure to be asked "the question" one more time. (Note that the females present were expected to fend for themselves. If they didn't, shame on them)

Such are the ingredients of family lore, pulled out and relished during holiday gatherings. May their number increase.

(c. 1980)

What's In a Name?
A Few More Like It

After spending both Holy Week and Easter Week in the company of relatives, first my side, then his, my husband and I felt compelled to tell our three that when the time came, we hoped they would choose not to give family names to their offspring.

The honor is lovely, but the confusion great. We pointed out a recent evening at the dinner table when three Andys (his side) figured in the conversation.

Later one of us suggested we should have tried Runyonese and distinguished them as San Juan Andy (the original), Princeton Andy (his son), and Niagara Falls Andy, also known as the Fuzz (nephew).

It's just as confusing on my side. There's my father Smethport Sam (original), Smethport Sam II (his son and my brother), and Rockland County Sam (grandson).

My father's father was Thomas.

This resulted in grandchildren Tommy, Tommy and Tommy (cousins with different fathers) and Thom, the last being my sister who turned out to be a girl but whose turn was up. She was christened Thomasina.

Back to my husband's family. His oldest brother is Mike. Mike is father to little Mike. Little Mike is now bigger than big Mike and I daresay that only family members still dare to call him Mikey.

My mother-in-law is Helen who sometimes answers to Nell. So is her daughter. They got around that one by calling Helen II, Honey. My husband was named Carmen after his father. They called him Butch to set him apart until he started fighting back.

My mother's name is Margaret, and every so often she can be heard fretting about her lack of namesakes. I tell her, politely, of course, she should cease and desist and be thankful she's one of a kind. She could have wound up with sisters bearing the same name as did San Juan Andy's daughters. All three are named Maria—Maria Elena, Maria Angela and Maria Christina, and in this instance, I'll have to admit, a bit of all right. (*Note: Mom did end up with a delightful namesake, one Margaret Allison Costa named for both of her grandmothers*)

Our children received non-family names. Johanna because it had grace and strength and meant God's gift. John became John for exactly the same reasons. Cara is Cara because in Italian it means Dear One and she was and is.

John, for one, shows signs of following the namesake tradition. Two years away from Confirmation he opined recently that when the time came he would take my brother Paul's name for the sacrament which he noted with glee would make him John Paul I. And his son, he explained needlessly, would someday be, what else?—John Paul II.

(c. 1980)

On Getting a New Pope

One of the first things that occurred to this writer upon hearing that we had a new Polish pope was the thought: Aha; this will take care of the infantile jokes.

It didn't of course. Polish jokes will be with us as long as there are small brains among us.

Such attempts at humor at the expense of an entire culture distress me a lot less than they once did, however.

When a nation can count as one of its own a man who is not only spiritual leader of 700 million people, but who also speaks nine languages as if they were his own, manages to convey love, compassion and humility in a single phrase and whose moral strength is matched only by his political clout, then that nation does not much need the defense of friends against drivel.

Some other thoughts on the selection:

If we rejoiced with the Poles for the elevation of this man to such heights, we must rejoice even more for ourselves. As Americans who have looked to Italians all our lives for our spiritual leadership in Rome, the choice of a non-Italian serves to remind us in the best possible way that we as Catholics are members of a universal faith, not as it has sometimes seemed, tied to a Church whose limits are defined by the Adriatic on one side and the Mediterranean on the other.

And how do Italians feel about the new Bishop of Rome?

I'm not sure. But I can tell you how one Italian-American responded. My father, somewhat biased when it comes to people, places and things Italian, had taken to John Paul I as all of us had, reading everything he could about him and praying for him daily.

"I don't know why," he would say. "There's something about him."

During a recent visit from Dad and Mom, I broached the subject of John Paul's successor.

How did he feel about this non-Italian with the hard-to-pronounce name filling the shoes of Albino Luciani? I waited for some polite words since my father is of the old school which sees the mildest criticism of any cleric akin to blasphemy.

There were no polite words. Dad's mouth softened, his eyes filled. "Ah, this one, this one," he crooned, "Even better."

(c. 1979)

The Bible – An Old Sun Rises Again

I am reading the bible, I tell a friend. For the first time. It is an embarrassing admission to make at my age. Not so much from religious aspects since only in recent years has reading it been stressed much in the Catholic Church.

Rather the chagrin comes from the fact that I, who have wanted to be a writer since age eight, have bypassed the richest of all literary sources.

I began six months ago with the grandiose plan of reading it straight through. Genesis zipped by. Exodus almost as easy. Bogged down with Leviticus. Mired in Numbers.

I flip ahead to Ecclesiastes, read Esther, Samuel, Ruth, Job in haphazard order. They charm, thrill, inspire, amuse. I turn back to Numbers determinedly and am stopped.

Furtively, (although no one cares but me that I am skipping) I jump into Proverbs. Proverbs is my cup of tea. I alternate it with the only part of the Bible previously familiar, the Gospels. In the quiet of the morning after the school buses leave, I sometimes weep over the beauty, the hope in certain familiar passages which seem to strike now with new clarity and promise.

Christmas approaches and with what I know to be euphoric zeal, I give Bibles as if they were bon bons. I debate over giving my father one. His reading has almost exclusively been the evening paper, super market manuals, seed catalogues and the Pennsylvania Fish and Game Magazine. He surprises us all.

By the end of January he is already up to Kings. Dad is aghast at the killings thus far. "Thirty thousand here, twenty thousand there," he says, and asks the question for which no one has an answer: "Why did God allow it?"   (c. 1980)

Housewife's Prayers

It occurred to me the other morning—and not for the first time—that I do not pray well on my knees.

As children we were trained to do so, to show reverence and, I suppose, as sort of a stimulus, the reasoning being that in that traditional position of supplication, the prayers would flow.

It is not as easy as that. Sometimes I make contact. Sometimes not. Not a formal person, it only follows that I am out of my milieu utilizing formal words and formal actions.

As a housewife of 16 years, I have discovered that there are other ways just as conducive as kneeling to communicating with the Lord.

One, almost guaranteed, is to stand alone in the kitchen, up to one's elbows in soapy dish water. I am not sure if it is the warmth of the water or the purging quality of the soap, but there have been lots of conversations held this way over the years, some of them fruitful.

Another is walking the dog in the cemetery, which except for caretakers and an occasional high school boy, sneaking a cigarette behind a large mausoleum, is usually deserted.

Driving alone in the car works fine, too, as does sitting on the passenger side as my husband drives in companionable silence.

There are other stimuli: watching our children sleep; pulling weeds with the hot summer sun on my back; listening to the burbling babies who sometimes share our pews.

And, of course, there is the provocation that does not start out as a prayer, but most certainly ends up as one.

"Lord, love a duck," I say in disgust as I unexpectedly walk on spilled sugar, find 32 wet towels in the hamper or catch somebody (or two somebodies) ice skating on the flag-stoned foyer. And, then, in earnest add, "And me too, please."

(c. 1980)

Hounding the Hound

A sign in front of a Protestant church caused me to do a double take recently. The title of the upcoming Sunday homily was, "Twisting the Lord's Arm." I was puzzled for a second, and then laughed out loud in recognition.

The first time I ever heard of putting pressure on the Lord, some 10 or 12 years ago, I gasped at the audacity of it. A visiting priest was on the altar. Tall, dark-haired and generally aloof, he was not one to inspire any great rapport with the congregation. Then he began to speak. I can't remember much of it. In fact only one line, "Trust in the Lord so implicitly," he said in his dry, toneless voice, "that you force him to answer your prayers."

Putting pressure on a human being was risky. Putting it on the Almighty had to be a fatal error.

I must have been waiting for him to be struck down in the pulpit. But, no when I looked up, he was beginning the Creed in the same toneless voice.

Over the years I've thought of that homilist more times than I can remember and for various reasons.

It gives me a strange kind of pleasure that the Lord frequently sees fit to deliver certain truths via people or incidents we don't find particularly engaging. It has something to do, I suppose, with keeping us receptive—and humble.

I also thought of that brusque-mannered priest every time I came across a couple of direct communiqués in the Gospels on the persistence of prayer.

I came to realize that far from being cheeky, "twisting the Lord's arm," is not only acceptable, but invited. I practice it daily, as I'm sure a lot of others do, all of us calling it by different names. In my case, it's known as hounding the Hound of Heaven.

(c. 1980)

Vive La Difference?

Our son, the French student, boarded a plane recently with some 20 other young Francophiles to study the language, culture and history of France. They would land in Brussels; go to Paris and later to Fontainebleau to stay with various families.

I gave him one last wave and thought how All-American he looked in his blue jeans, Levi's jacket and indoor soccer shoes.

Before agreeing to the trip arranged by the high school French Department, we discussed the benefits.

The opportunity to visit Normandy, the Loire Valley, Paris and other places was a chance of a lifetime. So we paid the money and signed a permission slip allowing him to drink wine with meals, as is the custom for young people in that country. We followed his itinerary via the schedule left with us and shortly after they left Paris and arrived in Fontainebleau, we telephoned him.

"Everything is awesome," our son reported. Paris was wonderful: He and a couple of friends had got lost taking the Metro (subway) out of town, but they had hopped another one and got back to their hotel before curfew. They'd visited the Louvre and seen the Mona Lisa, driven past the Moulin Rouge and gone to the Tour Eiffel and Arc de Triomphe. Best of all was shopping in the little shops along the Champs Elysee where one of the girls, who had visited France before, had taught them how to barter.

"None of us wanted to leave Paris," he said. " When it was time to go we cried and kissed and hugged each other." I looked at my husband. "Sounds like there was a little cultural wine drinking involved."

Our son continued his report. His French parents were marvelous and he and his roommate, Jeff, bought their French "mother" a teapot and cups for a birthday celebration and wished her "Bon Anniversaire." John was also speaking French to the hosts' three sons, none of whom spoke English.

We were impressed and as the days stretched on we became more excited as other communiqués from the travelers filtered through to us.

We went to pick John up at the airport at the appointed time. Half of the students were able to get an earlier flight home from New York. So it was only a small group which straggled off the plane.

Our son was about the fourth or fifth kid to hove into sight.

"Oh, my God," one of us said, no reverence intended. John wore the blue jeans but the Levi's jacket had been replaced with his beige dress jacket. On his head, tilted to one side was a white linen-like fedora. A gold chain about his throat completed the image.

Not until the next morning did we discover that he also had a hole in his left ear. (A fellow student had pierced it with the earring which she then lent to him.)

He left for school the next dressed in black with hat and earring.

My husband and I tried to be philosophical. Sometimes you get more than what you pay for.

(The high school French trip led to more study in Rennes during college. His grades were average, but his street French and his soccer skills became impressive. Discovered memorabilia: a hitherto undisclosed X-ray for a fractured collarbone.)

(c. 1985)

Cease and Desist, Mom

Our daughter warns me: "No more of those phony letters from college in your column. My friends all think I wrote them."

"But," I argue, "I was sure everybody would understand that I pieced the 'letters' together based on phone calls and letters home."

"Well they didn't," she says and tells me again to cease and desist.

It is not the first time one of our children has demanded I stop writing about them in this space. They have, for the last 14 years that the column has been in existence, been grist for the mill. And during that time they have made it clear that they would have much preferred the kind of mother who bakes cookies twice a week, can sew a Halloween or school play costume in half a day and do the laundry without losing half the socks.

I plead guilty to all their charges and when the aforementioned daughter sends

the following quote by George Orwell, I grin and acknowledge the truth therein.

"All writers are vain, selfish and lazy and at the very bottom of their motives there lies a mystery. Writing a book is a horrible, exhausting struggle, like a long bout of some painful illness. One would never undertake such a thing if one were not driven on by some demon whom one can neither resist nor understand."

Accompanying the quote is her explanation of how she thought it appropriate reading for someone who continues to turn out a novel a year and still has to see one published.

Since receiving the note, I have been trying to figure out why I continue to write in the face of rejection.

One reason is that I have had enough encouraging notes from editors to keep me going. Ditto the veteran authors in our writing group who point out that persistence is the name of the game.

But those reasons alone are

not sufficient to keep pounding out words. Over the last five years with three drafts per book I have produced well over a million words, none of them profound.

So what is the reason? I'm not sure myself, but undoubtedly part of it is that I enjoy the escape.

And, part of it is also the opportunity to create and control one's characters. How satisfying to sit down and give birth to people who won't talk back to you and whom you can make as villainous, heroic or nutty as you like.

Likewise it is fun to create dialogue particularly for a confrontation and have the characters say things to each other you've never dared voice in real life.

George Orwell to the contrary, writing can be great fun. It certainly beats housework.

Three years after this column appeared my first book was published. Not one of the six romances I'd slaved over, but a young adult novel populated with characters much like those who inhabit our home.

(c. 1984)

A Mystery Solved

I have been trying to find the name of the first book that my mother ever read to me. Apparently taking me into her bed and reading was a ploy to get me to sleep. Instead Mom would nod off and I would take up the book and finish "reading" it—or so the recounting went.

The problem in trying to locate the book was that I knew neither the title nor the author. I did, however, remember that there were three kittens, Fluff, Muff and Algernon. Later a writer friend who had the same book told me that the kittens in question had been dressed in clothing. That seemed to fit. But she couldn't remember the title either.

My quest had a certain poignancy. During my mother's last days when she drifted in and out of consciousness, my father sat by her bedside taking down every word she muttered. Later he showed me the small notebook. "I figured these two out, but couldn't get this last one," he said. He had Fluff and

Muff, but he had been unable to decipher Algernon.

Over the years I hunted for the book sporadically mentioning the characters' names to friends, to clerks at used book stores and more recently even to an antique dealer who had quite a few old picture books. No one knew the title or author. Then friends suggested I try Google, the search engine, and look for books published in the mid-thirties.

Actually I used HotBot my (then) favorite search engine and came up with a wonderful site called Loganberry's, a bookstore in Cleveland. And there I found a section devoted to stumping the bookseller. People emailed the site with questions such as "What was the name of the book in which an old lady lived in a treehouse?" Answer: "Miss Twiggly's Tree." (I mention this one because I gave our children's copy away and had to search and buy another for 10 times the price when our older daughter wanted to read it to her children.)

Scrolling down the many, many questions at the Loganberry site I came across "Four Little Kittens." It was obviously a popular book as many people had inquired about it. It seems I had forgotten about the fourth kitten, Puff. And the book, Four Little Kittens, was the work of a photographer, Harry Whittier Frees, who dressed up the animals in clothing. He did companion books starring puppies and rabbits. Loganberry's did not have a copy of Four Kittens but a used book site, www.bookfinders.com listed several, some of them reissues. Because there were several books about the kittens' activities, and I have not determined which I had, I've yet to order it. The prices listed are another stumbling block. One copy is advertised at $75. The thought, however, of meeting Fluff, Muff, Puff and Algernon once again is a tempting one.

There is another problem. According to one correspondent to the site, the book was about bunnies named Fluff, Muff, Puff and Algernon. The kittens, who were neighbors of the bunnies, had other names including Agamemnon. Now I'm really confused. If anyone remembers such characters, please write .

As it turned out, someone did respond. I was wrong about the characters, Muff, Fluff and Algernon being kittens. They were indeed rabbits although the author/photographer did produce a book about kittens.

(c. 2000)

Hitchin' A Ride

Friends and relatives are flying all over the place. One heads for Paris, another for California, a third to Florida. I yearn for another trip to Italy, but hang back. In the past 25 years or so flying has been problematic for me. Events of receny years have acerbated my anxiety.

My first flight, if I remember correctly, was in 1958 or thereabouts, My younger sister Thomasina, who was newly wed, and I flew from Mt. Alton, a tiny airport on top of a mountain near our home in northwest Pennsylvania to NYC. The airlines was Allegheny out of Pittsburgh and our plane, a DC3, a converted transport carrier. I don't remember much about the trip other than we sat in conventional seats, and it was so warm my sister had to use the provided paper bag at least once.

The return trip was much better. The empty interior of the cargo plane was ice cold and instead of passenger seats, there was a long metal bench that ran along one side, luggage on the floor at our feet. There were no seat belts and I don't think there were any other passengers either. For some reason, I felt very safe in that plane. A year or so later I took a similar flight to Rochester to start a new job with the daily newspaper when snow and ice prevented my driving. Planes stopped flying into Mt. Alton in the mid-sixties after one crashed and burned on the mountain

As a young general assignment reporter I had another memorable flying experience in the early sixties. A thousand Marines took part in a mock invasion, landing on the Lake Ontario beach at Charlotte. I was assigned to do a first-person story which entailed riding in one of the choppers. Imagine my surprise when I found myself sitting on a bench in the middle of a bunch of young macho men directly opposite an open door which remained that way throughout the short flight.

This time, happily, belts were in order. Instead of jumping to the ground as the Marines did I dropped into a pair of uniformed arms. All in all an interesting assignment!

In those early flights, I had little or no fear. Not until I had children did I become irrational about flying. For some reason the bigger , more sophisticated, more crowded the plane, the less sanguine I was about the outcome.

On our first family trip to Italy in the mid-seventies our kids were delirious with happiness. I spent the entire time clutching the arm rests, and about 2 a.m. when the Alps were visible and everybody rushed to the right of the plane for a good look, I was sure the imbalance would down us.

Our children are grown now and fly hither and yon on their own, but their mother's fear still remains, heightened by the terrorist threat. After giving it much thought I've figured out that all I have to do to allay my fears is figure out how to hitch a ride on a government cargo plane to Rome or Milan. In my case, perception is everything.

(c. 2004)

Cabbage And?

"Don't forget to wear your green," said the head of the house this past Sunday, as we were dressing for church. Forget the fact that the other 360 plus days of the year he celebrates his Italian names and heritage.

Silently I put on my green— not too hard a chore when everything I own is green anyway including several jackets, winter coat, spring coat, fall coat, etc. More importantly I knew it would make this son of the former Helen Fitzgerald happy to see me garbed in the color of the day. A small enough thing to do, I thought, even if all my ancestors came from Italy.

The day before as we trawled the aisles of the supermarket, I'd come across a woman handing out samples of corned beef and cabbage. As it was nearing lunch time I asked for and received a small cup of a dark brown mixture of meat bits and vegetables cooked to a fare-thee-well.

If there is anything less appetizing than overcooked vegetables, I am not sure what it is. However, I am a cabbage lover and when I saw the firm heads at a good price in an adjacent stall, I picked out a small one

A friend of mine married to a man straight from the "auld sod" once told me that in Ireland the dish is cabbage and *ham*. "Don't know anything about corned beef," she'd said. That set the stage for me to go to the meat counter and choose a chunk of turkey ham, my husband eating neither beef nor pork the past 20 years.

A cursory glance at a cookbook and I was off and running the next night. Potato, carrots, onion. Steamed them in a little water, then added the cabbage. First mistake: potato was a bit mushy by the time the cabbage was cooked. Added chunks of the turkey ham and put the heat on low so the flavors could marry at which time I discovered my second mistake. I'd started the whole thing too early and the

"Irishman" was still enjoying his Pinot Grigio.

We sat down a half hour later and when seconds were requested, I figured I'd passed the big test. Silently I sent up thanks to his mother Helen (Nell) who was certainly looking down from above in amusement and understanding. After all, the daughter of Big Tim Fitzgerald, who had initially opposed her marriage to an Italian, had learned to cook ziti and sausage with a masterful hand.

(c. 2002)

A Taste of Extravaganza

For my birthday, my husband gave me a copy of "The Story of English," a companion to the PBS television series written by Robert McCrum, William Cran and TV reporter Robert MacNeil. The gift, by far the handsomest and most expensive of our books on language, brought our total to a baker's dozen.

I dipped eagerly into the heavy, glossy pages replete with color illustrations and maps, spurred on by the blurb which noted that 350 million people around the world use it as their mother tongue.

Skipping from a discourse on the English spoken in Appalachia to one on the contributions of black jazzmen, to a piece on Mark Twain, I leaped to the contributions made by foreign tongues to the English language.

As an American of Italian extraction I was eager to see what my forebears had contributed. With some dismay and a lot of amusement, I read that the "influence of Italian words is mainly limited to food words such as pizza, spaghetti, lasagna, espresso, ravioli…"

I felt that my Italian immigrant grandparents, passionate Yankees all, would not want me to take that lying down. Particularly because words are my business, and my love. I was certain our ancestors must have contributed something besides multisyllabic dishes and our country's name (Americus Vespucci) to the vocabulary.

Without even trying, a whole segment of Italian contributions leaped to mind. How could these learned gentlemen have missed them? The answer was obvious. McCrum, Cran and MacNeil thought that opera, maestro and piano were exotic foods.

The same for forte, prima donna, crescendo, coloratura, soprano, diva, segue, sonata, stanza, tempo, vibrato, cello and viola and a couple hundred more musical terms.

I stayed in the arts: Gesso, studio, tempera, sienna, terrazzo, sepia, patina, fresco, cartoon (from cartone) chiaroscuro, caricature. To the untutored ear, Italian pastries? Maybe.

But what about ballerina, gala, extravaganza, fantasia, literati, novella, scenario, stanza, terza rima? Nobody could confuse them with foods... No, wait...extravaganza...a dessert cheese? Yes, that's it—milder than gorgonzola, with a little more bite than mozzarella.

Ghetto? Fiasco? Cognoscenti? Credenza, graffiti, inferno, influenza, madonna, malaria, gondola? Well, it's possible the authors forgot about them. After all, how often do we hear these esoteric examples? Ditto for ditto and other such rarities as motto, sequin, incognito, carnival, replica, umbrella, volcano and zero.

With this small sampling whetting my appetite, I can hardly wait to delve into the rest of the book. I plan to devour it, if you'll pardon the expression, with gusto.

(1986)

The Gulf War

Some thoughts as I watch our younger daughter seal two letters for her sailor husband in the Gulf, dabbing on each a bit of perfume that he gave her before he left. Inside are the latest pictures of their baby, Angel Jr.

The war that we thought, hoped and prayed would not happen is a fact, its horrors transmitted almost instantaneously to our living rooms. Each day some new obscenity causes us to recoil and the experts tell us that more surprises are coming.

The TV pictures underscore another truth: War is started by men with pesky prostates and quivering jowls who send the fresh-faced, the country's hope, to do their dying for them.

Herbert Hoover didn't need TV to know that. In a speech at the Republican National Convention of 1944 he noted: Older men declare war. But it is youth that must fight and die. And it is youth who must inherit the tribulation, the sorrow and the triumphs that are the aftermath of war."

It is hard to see what triumphs there can be in this war or indeed any war.

William Tecumseh Sherman didn't think there were. "I am sick and tired of war," he told a graduating class, Michigan Military Academy in 1879. "Its glory is all moonshine. It is only those who have neither fired a shot nor heard the shrieks and groans of the wounded who cry aloud for blood, more vengeance, more desolation. War is hell."

About those who feel that the media should be restricted and government allowed total censorship.

One wonders how long the Viet Nam War might have gone on had not newsmen such as Walter Cronkite and others refused to take the government handouts and instead found generals who were willing to tell the truth.

(2/1991)

Company We Love

It's that time of year. We pulled out the trundle bed, borrowed another crib, fired up the grill and checked our list of tourist attractions. It is the season for visitors.

It began in June when my husband's brother, Andrew, sister-in-law Betsy and niece, Cara II (our daughter is Cara I) arrived from Puerto Rico by way of Albany where they had been staying with author Bill Kennedy, an old friend and newspaper colleague of Andrew's.

Knowing that Kennedy, whose house guests often include other famous authors, offers scintillating wit and conversation, we tried to come up with equally diverting entertainment.

We figured we could top him by bringing out our own five-star attraction, our 21-month old grandson, but alas A.J. went camping that particular weekend with his other grandparents.

But all was not lost. Neither Cara II or Betsy had ever gone picking strawberries so early on Saturday morning we took ourselves to a local field where we picked, ate and snapped pictures to mark the historic event. Later in the day nephew, Andy, and his wife Michelle pulled in from Lewiston.

A week later, our son-in-law came home from the Gulf, his carrier, the Ranger, taking the round-about way back. Angel divided his time between our house and his parents and got reacquainted with his son.

He left three weeks later and my sister Judy, her husband Mike and Christopher, 4, and Peter, 2, from Cornwall, NY hove in a few days afterward. Judy who has been visiting here since childhood, needs no entertainment. She packed up her crew and went to the Corn Hill festival, took long drives and in between made good use of the pool.

They pulled out Sunday before noon. Thirty minutes later niece Eve, with Alissa 5 and

Timothy, 15 months, arrived from Rockland County. Eve who'd visited a couple of years before with niece, Ann, and Ann's son Johnny, knew her way around and visited our malls, took her kids to Charlotte beach and the carousel and in between chasing kids, sunbathed around the pool.

Through all this, I maintained my daily schedule at the computer, made possible by the fact that all our guests were laid back, willing to cook and otherwise help out. Judy made a scrumptious dish combining small zucchini, clams and linguine. Betsy made our favorite Puerto Rican beans and rice and Eve pitched in one night to create a huge pizza.

Weren't there some hairy moments? Relatively few (pun intended). Granted, the housekeeping standards, never very high, were relaxed further. There was an occasional squabble over a toy. But on the whole, the get-togethers were memorable fun reunions.

(7/1991)

Christmas at Our House

A true story by A.J. Santiago, 7, as told to Grandma

On the 12th day before Christmas we put up our tree—and Sheba, our cat, jumped up on it and knocked it over.

On the 11th day before Christmas we went to the mall and…Austie screamed when it was his turn to talk to Santa.

On the tenth day of Christmas Mommy and I made cut-out cookies—And in the middle of the night Clem, our dog, ate them All!

On the ninth day of Christmas we made more cookies—And Clem threw up on the living room carpet.

On the eighth day before Christmas we got the wreath from the attic...And a mouse crawled out.

On the seventh day before Christmas we wrote and sent out cards—and the mail truck got stuck in front of our house.

On the sixth day before Christmas we made red punch with green cherries and Uncle Harry told Army stories for six hours straight.

On the fifth day before Christmas Grandma cooked squid (that's octopus!) because her grandmother always did… and Grandpa took us all out for pizza.

On the fourth day before Christmas we went caroling and Uncle Harry sang in Z flat.

On the third day of Christmas we gave a big party—and a blizzard came and all the company had to sleep over—three of them in my bed.

On the second day before Christmas we decorated the tree again ..and the cat (well you know the rest.)

On the day before Christmas we hung up our stockings… and Austie filled mine with Hershey's syrup.

On Christmas day we opened

presents, sang Happy Birthday to Baby Jesus and Grandpa got misty-eyed while Grandma kissed every one of us ten times (even Uncle Harry). Because that's what Christmas is all about.

(1996)

Hooked On Gettysburg

Conventional wisdom to the contrary, you can not only teach an old dog new tricks, e.g. how to make the most of one's computer, but you can also get him (and her) interested in new subjects.

In high school I was eager to skip over the Civil War with its bloody recounting of battles and horrendous number of casualties. And in all the years that followed, I saw nothing to change my opinion that this American conflict, fought on American soil, was something I cared to delve into. Yes, someday I would visit Gettysburg and take one or more young grandsons along to give them an idea of what our nation had endured 140 years ago.

Then in October on a short sojourn to the beautiful, restored Inner Harbor in Baltimore, my husband and I decided on the way back to make a stop at Gettysburg. On a warm Fall day, the crowds were very large, but apparently not as overwhelming as they are on a summer weekend.

We stopped first at the Visitor Center which reinforced my original feelings about the conflict. Wall after wall of young men's splotchy images greet visitors, their bleak gazes seeming to meet mine. Below in an atrium were display cases of rifles. At one counter, tours of battlefields and Ike and Mamie's retirement farmhouse were being hawked. I escaped into an adjacent area where books and other paraphernalia were being sold. Cash registers merrily rang up huge totals as visitors, some of whom had traveled long distances, couldn't seem to get enough memorabilia. I overheard one expert behind the counter advise against buying the pseudo bullets on display. "Two tons of ammunition were fired in three days," he said. "You can get the real thing for your kids at a nearby store."

Quickly we left the center and walked across the road to the cemetery where rows of veterans now lay, trying to figure out the exact spot where President Lincoln gave his address. I was ready to find a motel, but my husband suggested a quick ride through the meadows that became battlefields. Happy to be away from the center where death and suffering are commodities to be sold and treasured, I agreed, the events of Sept. 11 a mere month behind us undoubtedly playing a part in the revulsion I felt.

We rode slowly past the now infamous wheat field, through the peach orchard and then up to Little Round Top and got out of the car. Down and across from us was Devil's Den similar, if smaller, to the rock city on the hill behind my father's house in northwest Pennsylvania. We walked around, touched trees, examined boulders, speculating as to positions the men took to exchange shots. Gradually I understood the pull that the Battle of Gettysburg has on so many people including my brother Sam and cousins Pam and Greg, who visit once a year from their home near Pittsburgh.

At home, the next day, I headed for the library gathering up an armload of books including some written for young readers, always a way to get a succinct, easily grasped hold on a subject. And we rented the excellent 1993 film, *Gettysburg*. By far the best source was Pulitzer Prize winner Bruce Catton's final book, *"Reflections on the Civil War."*

This past Sunday night I was browsing with the remote before heading for bed and book, and came across Jimmy Stewart in *Shenandoah*, a sentimental offering about a Virginia farmer during the Civil War. Ordinarily I would have passed it up. Instead I burrowed further into the couch and watched a good half hour, reluctantly admitting that when it came to the Civil War, I, too, was now hooked.

(2002)

What's with November?

Some years ago during the month of November, my husband went to the doctor with a vague complaint. He wasn't feeling up to par. The doctor consulted his file, looked up at him and said, "The last time you came to see me was in November. And the time before that—was November." The doctor looked at my husband and said, "Something traumatic must have happened to you one November. What was it?"

My husband blurted out the first thing that came to him. "I got married," he said.

We laughed when he first recounted that story and I laugh whenever I think of it still. This past week we marked our 26th anniversary and the longer we are married, the more I applaud the doctor for his shrewd question, and my husband for his spontaneous, honest answer.

At 28 and 31 we were not lovesick kids, but two adults who knew what we wanted, i.e., someone with compatible interests, background, goals, values. I'm not sure I analyzed it that way, at first. All I knew was that being with him was like coming home, finding a safe harbor where I enjoyed an incredible sense of well-being and warmth. The harbor was also a port from which we both could venture out, broaden our horizons, knowing the other would be there on our return, to praise, encourage and, if necessary, salve the wounds.

For all these years we have attempted to mesh two distinct personalities, two egos, two sets of doubts and vulnerabilities. For every subject we agree on, there is another we don't. He is city born and bred, I am country. The mighty Hudson River/winding Marvin Creek. Fine china on starched linen/ a mug of coffee over a smoky campfire. Ernest Hemingway/ Jane Austen. Private prayers over community witnessing. Small Christmas celebrations/ family extravaganzas. And on and on and on.

So what is keeping us going? Habit? The children who no longer need us but whose binding force continues? In part. And part is the quickening inside me that still occurs each night when the door opens and he walks in.

(1989)

Growing Up, Growing Away

When Johanna, the oldest of our three children, turned five I wrote a poem for the occasion—something to do with her growing up and growing away from us.

Her father, upon reading it, snorted at the maudlin tone. "Good grief, you sound as if she was getting married and leaving home." I remember turning away so he would not see my face. To me every birthday of each child represented a threat to the family circle.

A couple of Saturdays ago— 17 1/2 years after that particular birthday—Johanna and Ron were married and I felt only happiness. Granted my eyes did fill just before she and her father came down the aisle at St. Joseph's but I always cry when I hear the *Ave Maria*. And a mother can be forgiven for thinking her daughter beautiful in her bride's dress I suppose, but then I've always thought her

so even in wet diapers or filthy soccer uniform.

She and her husband left that night for a wedding trip to the West Coast and when they returned they went to their new apartment, leaving the blue bedroom she had occupied the last 15 years, empty, except for a closet full of textbooks and one barely used dress of tulle and lace.

I looked in, waiting for the tears to come then. Instead I congratulated myself that she, who had insisted on going to a college seven hours away, had married a hometown boy who lives in this area.

"You'd be singing another tune if she were moving to California," a friend said.

No doubt. Nor would her father and I have been so laid back about her marriage had we not loved and respected her husband as we do. The only boyfriend she ever had or wanted, Ron came into her life six years ago as her soccer coach, and stayed to become her best friend, her ally and confidante, her partner. Would that every parent's child find so kind, so steadfast a mate!

Yet with all these pluses to the marriage, it still seemed as if I should have "grieved more at losing her" as one acquaintance put it.

I've thought about it off and on for the last month. The answer, when it came, was something I've known (but not admitted) for years.

Johanna began leaving home a long time ago. The first time was at 10 months when her father took her with him to run Saturday errands, leaving me at loose ends. The next was when she was almost three and ran alone across the yard to play at a neighbor's, stopping once to turn and wave as I stood in the doorway to make sure she arrived safely.

Over the years, her journeys have grown longer, more frequent. Each time her father and I watched to see that she had "arrived safely." Upon one return—neither of us can remember just which one—she came home an adult, fully and demonstrably capable of taking charge of her life. Maybe we cried then. But I don't think so. It was, after all, what we had –in spite of my lapses—set out to do.

(1987)

Darling Clementine

In this space last issue, my husband, standing in for me, described the loss of our pet and family member, Clementine, and suggested I would have more to say in future columns. I did not intend to do so so quickly, but it seemed important, to stress not Clem's passing but the 15 years of her life granted to us. I also felt compelled to write about our son who brought me through a tough time.

Everyone loved Clementine, but no one more than John. Clem was brought home as a birthday present for our animal-loving youngest, Cara, who turned 7 a week before Christmas 1976. But it was her older brother, John, 9, whose sense of wonder and delight over the tiny creature knew no bounds.

When the black ball of fur kept us awake the first night, crying for her mother and siblings, when puddles appeared elsewhere than on the spread-out papers, and when Clem jumped and snatched candy canes off the tree that first Christmas, John crooned, "Baaad dog, baad dog." The dulcet, adoring tones gave the lies to his words, causing his father and me more than once to hide our smiles behind cupped hands.

The only boy in the family, John slept in his own room at the end of the hall, besieged by nightmares and the "monsters" growing out of the woodgrain on his closet doors. His sisters, Johanna and Cara, had each other's beds to run to in thunderstorms or after a scary TV show, but John felt alone and bad dreams often disturbed his sleep. His father frequently made the trip down the hall in John's early years to soothe him.

As soon as Clem was trained, she slept at the end of his bed and John was no longer alone. A mutt that was supposed to be part water spaniel and part Irish spaniel, it was soon clear that a black lab lurked somewhere in her ancestry. Resembling a miniature thoroughbred as she flew across the yard on racehorse legs, she grew to a large size, sometimes sleeping on John's feet. Ungrumbling, he would move to accommodate her hefty, albeit graceful, 75 pounds.

When Clem was 8, John went off to college, but still every night she made the trips upstairs to sleep at the bottom of his bed. He spent his junior year in France, coming home after the long absence, to be greeted by a wildly excited Clem. Later he would go away for weeks at a time, returning always to kiss first his tail-thumping "Puppy," as he called her, and then his mother.

Always sensitive to Clem's desire to be in the midst of the family, John felt her frustration when she could no longer negotiate the stairs she had once so blithely floated up and down, and carried her up to be with the rest of us at night.

On the Monday night I realized how sick Clem was, I called the vet who suggested I bring her in. Torn about taking her to a place she was so frightened of, I dithered. It was John, home at 11, who insisted I call the vet back. Now a 6-footer, he gently picked Clem up and cradled her in his arms,

soothing her as he carried her to the darkened car, strong when I was not.

And it was John who brought Clem home for the last time, her covered form resting on the narrow truck seat next to him. He climbed out, his composure breaking once. When I wavered over where he would lay her, he said in soft reproach, tears in his eyes, "You know, Mom, this isn't getting any easier."

With the help of his father and a neighbor, John buried our dog and later that night, this most openly tender-hearted of our children, asked if he could have Clem's ID tag.

Afterward, the picture of John, the gentle, strong adult cradling and soothing the sick, old dog fused with that of the frightened child comforted by the solid warmth of the new puppy.

It was clear some time ago, our son had completed the journey from boy to man, but never more evident than now that he'd been helped through the passage by this loving and beloved creature of God.

(Nov. 6 1991)

(Note to Reader: See fictional story Upon a Winter's Night.)

Dog Talk

My mother never told me not to talk to strangers. (Probably because she did it all the time herself). And for that I am glad. Otherwise, I'd miss out on some of life's diverting moments.

I was at the bank this past week, inside instead of my usual stop at the driveup window. The line was long and the woman behind me, a stately six-footer in sweats which contrasted with her freshly coifed white hair, exchanged a grimace over the delay.

We looked away and then as the delay continued, she murmured something about having come from her aerobics class and passing her hairdresser's on the way. This stop was definitely not going as well.

I mentioned that walking was my workout of choice except when the weather was poor.

"I often walk," she replied, "in order to exercise my dog."

"Well, I always did, too," I told her, but I lost my dog at age 15 two years ago."

"That's when I lost mine too," she aid, "And it was lonely. So I went up to Lollypop Farm, not meaning to get a dog, mind you, but just to visit with some of them. And I spotted this one and, well, I don't know. I just took to him."

"I keep thinking about getting another dog, but I'm not ready to let another one in," I admitted. "They take hold of you so completely and then I worry about them just as if they were one of my kids."

She nodded agreement and continued, "And so I took him home and he's just the best company. He'd been neglected, but he was a good dog and there was just something in his look—he's a boxer—that I couldn't resist."

The line was nudging along. I hesitated only briefly, then confided: "I miss my dog so much. So I sometimes dogsit for my neighbors. "She nodded understanding.

By that time, I was up to the window and moved to take

care of business. As luck would have it, we both finished at the same time, meeting again at the swinging glass doors and walking out into the fall sunshine together.

"By the way, what's your dog's name?" I asked.

She grinned. "I named him Mike Tyson. A boxer, you know. Then Tyson had all the bad publicity and I didn't want all the teasing, so I call him Mike."

I laughed and told her I'd enjoyed talking with her. She waved and we drove off in our respective cars, I thinking how sad if I'd missed that day brightener because I'd been taught otherwise.

The encounter reminded me of a story about a woman in her late 80's whose enjoyment of life and easy adjustment to advancing age was clear to see. When asked her secret, she said it was because along the way she'd learned that losing friends to death, to moves and other changes was a part of life.

Thus, she kept making new friends by taking advantage of every opportunity that came her way. It was the new friends who kept her interested in life and her life interesting.

(1993)

A Horror Story?

When our dog Clem was alive, the squirrels annoyed her and us from sunup to sundown. Not only did they empty the birdfeeders of every last seed but they teased Clem relentlessly.

She would run from the sliding glass door in the kitchen to the one in the sunroom/office barking madly as they cavorted deliberately in her view, aware she was unable to give chase.

Then our beloved Clem died and the house and the yard were unbearably quiet.

When a cardinal or raucous blue jay visited, I was overjoyed and would throw out toast crumbs or break up a stale cookie on the patio.

In no time the squirrels were back in full force.

Exasperation gave way to amusement as I watched these pesky creatures, perched on hind legs, nibbling on a crumb. Then one day, fearful that a slab of chocolate cake that had been on the counter for a couple of days would make its way into my mouth, I threw it out. The boldest of the bushy tail pack grabbed it and fled to a low limb of the sycamore.

A leftover pancake, sailed Frisbee-style, was followed a couple of days later by a chunk of corn bread. The squirrels loved it all and I began think what a cute children's picture book this might make.

The book idea grew as I discovered a small dish of leftover spaghetti in the fridge.

I couldn't help myself. It went out the back door and the boldest squirrel had the whole family roaring as it perched on its hind legs threading a long strand through its paws to its greedy mouth.

"You'd better watch it," my husband warned. "You don't know what kind of rodent you'll get next."

So I made sure that I threw out treats in the middle of the day and only enough for the resident squirrels.

Then one weekend we were gathered around the round kitchen table, when a face appeared at the corner of the sliding glass door, asking "Where's Mine?" Up close it was easy to see that the squirrel had a cleft in its left ear. Rewarding its boldness, one of us grabbed a crust of bread and threw it out on the lawn. From time to time, the squirrel would come to the door to beg.

But one day it refused to go away. Sitting on the back of the patio bench, it watched our every move through the glass doors. With two small grandsons visiting often, I became nervous. What if the animal, now named Pirate thanks to its scruffy look and audacious manner, tried to get in the house? I tried shooing it away as did my daughters. Pirate barely budged. I got the broom and shook it in its face. No success.

One afternoon I was at my computer upstairs next to a closed window. Suddenly Pirate was high in the sycamore branches which brush against the house. He then flung himself against the window, holding onto the screen, staring me in the face. I banged on the window, but he refused to move.

Just as I thought of the sharp teeth it must have, Pirate opened his mouth. The small fangs were long, yellow and sharp. And with that he took a bite out of the screen. I ran downstairs and got a stick. By the time I was back he had torn away a large chunk of mesh; his body insinuated between the screen and glass. I pounded on the window enough to make him retreat to the tree. Now I was alarmed.

A call to wildlife control brought a helpful attendant with a Have-a-Heart trap. At his suggestion I baited it with peanut butter. The next day Pirate managed to get the food out from the side without springing the trap.

Later we caught a chipmunk which I freed. Pirate robbed the trap several times more. At the end of the week, we had trapped and freed a frantic blackbird while Pirate had amused himself, and frightened me, by attaching himself to the screen at the sliding glass door.

Another call to wildlife control brought a bigger trap and the comment, "Don't be surprised if you catch a raccoon."

Praying I wouldn't, I again baited the trap. The next day we had a squirrel—but not Pirate. Wildlife Control came to take it away and release it elsewhere and left another trap, but I was not hopeful. This sadder, but wiser, animal lover will keep trying.

As to the children's book? "Forget it Mom," our younger daughter Cara advised. "Pirate is definitely a Steven King character. Try a horror story."

(c. 1993)

St. Paul at Tres Tabernae

(**This was written early in 2000 when the magic of the internet first became apparent.**)

The most recent example of how wondrous it is to research online came as I was working on *Growing Up Italian in God's Country.* It is difficult to find anything on small towns in Italy, particularly those south of Rome -- in travel books or elsewhere. So I keystroked in Cisterna, the name of the town, some 35 miles southeast of Rome from where my maternal grandfather emigrated at age 19 in 1910.

Up came an arcane site all about some computer gadgetry. However, there was the name and e-mail address of someone in Cisterna. I immediately e-mailed him and asked a question or two. A young man, a college student, one Giampaolo Noto replied but when I responded with a lengthier question there

was no answer and I thought I'd discouraged him as his English, while far better than my Italian, was sketchy.

Then a week or so ago while studying a map and remember the gray, brooding mountain we'd seen while driving away from Cisterna down Rt. 7, which is the old Appian Way, I decided to try emailing again. Was the mountain visible on our left Monti Lepini?

Within 24 hours came a reply about the mountain and much more. The mountain, indeed, was Monti Lepini, the limestone element responsible for the bleak appearance. The towns at its foot were Cori, Norma, Sezze etc. The first is famous for its "palio", a horserace similar to that held in Siena, and for a newly proclaimed saint, Tommaso of Cori. Cisterna, Giampaolo wrote, is also famous for its butteri, (cowboys) and Cisterna is mentioned in the bible.

The cowboy fame I'd heard before. In 1985 when my husband and I traveled by cab from Sorrento where our tour was staying to Bellona where he discovered some cousins, the cabbie had mentioned that Cisterna was famous for its horsemen. And as it turned out this summer, I became the tentative holder of a large framed picture of a great-uncle Raffaele in a WWI uniform astride a horse.

According to Giampaolo, one of Cisterna's "cowboys" Augusta Imperiali or the Great Augustus had bested our Buffalo Bill in some contest.

But the information that sent me scrambling to several versions of the Bible was the line that Cisterna was the Tres Tabernae in Acts, 28:15. On Paul's journey to Rome, the author of Acts writes that Christians hearing of his impending arrival in the city came as far as Tres Tabernae and Appi Forum to meet them.

Tres Tabernae is most often translated Three Taverns but my dictionary also gave inn and hut as translations. Appi Forum was the Appian marketplace.

Studying various maps of Paul's journeys, and then present day maps of the Appian Way with Cisterna and nearby Velletri marked, I was fairly sure that Giampaolo was on target. But I wanted to see it confirmed elsewhere.

On a recent Sunday I found a small stool in the religion corner of a new bookstore and began opening books, studying each index. On the fourth try in a volume titled, "Nelson's Illustrated Encyclopedia of Bible Facts," I found Cisterna, with the notation that it was the Three Taverns mentioned in Acts. Actually it said "near Cisterna" but that was good enough for me.

Note that my confirmation source, one I respected, came in the form of printed material. The point is that the Internet is a wonderful new tool, one that works best with that other earlier miracle, the printing press.

(c. 2000)

Finding
Great-Grandmother

A short while ago I wrote of the wonders of the Internet for research, e.g., the Social Security Death Index. A night or so before the column appeared, the announcement I'd long been waiting for was made on ABC. Ellis Island records of the millions of immigrants who had passed through its gates were being made public.

The site:

www.ellisislandrecords.org.

With a yip of exultation I raced upstairs to my computer and got the same message that millions of other TV listeners got that night, i.e. the site was receiving many visitors. Please try again.

I did. Oh, I did. At two a.m. At 6 a.m. At midnight. I wanted to see my great-grandparents and grandfathers' names. No luck. Then five days later in spring, 2001 I learned why. Again ABC had the story. The site had received some 50 million hits

in the first six hours it was operating. Genealogy is among the top pastimes in the United States. The site is invaluable to both the scholarly researcher and the mildly curious. It tells not only the name, but age, occupation, city or region and country of origin and the port of departure. Then, if you get to the next screen, you can find the name of the ship on which they sailed. If you get to succeeding screens, you can see the original manifest and a drawing of the ship.

Eventually I found my great-grandmother. Or I think I did. Having consulted a series edited by Glazier and Filby titled, "Italians to America" at the Rochester Central Library, I'd found her name a year or so ago. Italian women and other Europeans retain their maiden name. My grandmother's maiden name was Vittoria Casa. I found Vittoria Caso.

Directly underneath were the four children who accompanied her, surname Policastro, with thee of the four ages on target, two of the names close. (Great-grandfather Giuseppe Policastro who arrived in 1891 was processed at Castle Garden, Ellis Island not opening until the next year). When I finally was able to access the site, the information was the same except the children's surname transcribed by Mormon Church members as (Poliastro), i.e. missing the c. I decided nevertheless that I'd found them. Ships' officers who took down the names were notoriously lax and if two sets of transcribers could differ on spellings, then no doubt other mistakes were made.

The biggest thrill so far is finding my husband's father's name. My husband's grandmother had been living here and went back to Bellona, Italy to give birth then returned when the infant was a couple months old. In this case, the child was listed with both his mother and father's surnames with his age unknown.

I already had naturalization papers for both my Costa and Borelli grandfathers and knew the years they came, the names of the ships, port of departure, length of journey etc. Still I couldn't find them.

One reason I couldn't find Grandpa Tom Costa was that there were thousands of Costas listed. Was he Thom, Tomas or Tommaso? Eventually I just used the initial T and found him. It was Tommaso which I'd been spelling incorrectly. I've still to find Grandma Maria Concetta Costa who came two years later. Her maiden name: Corcoglioniti. I also have yet to find my maternal grandfather Pasquale Borelli despite the fact that I have all the pertinent info listed on his naturalization papers. He came over alone as a boy of 19 in 1910. There are many with the name Pasquale Borelli in the records, but none is the right age or date. I can hardly wait to see how he was listed. Perhaps he used his first initial and middle name Giovanni. Whatever he used, I will be thrilled when I do make the connection.

The site for me continues to be the most fascinating on the Internet. It is still impossible to access it at various times of the day. The best: early Sunday morning. Half of the U.S. population is sleeping in.

The other half is in church.

As luck would have it, just prior to publishing "Growing Up Italian in God's Country" in September 2001 I was able to access a screen which showed passenger destinations. There amid the Chicago, New York and other metropolitan destinations was Vittoria's objective : Davis, Pa., a hamlet of a few houses in the Tioga County wilderness where Great-grandfather was working on a logging railroad. I had found my great-grandmother.

Note: In September, 2005 I found Grandpa Borelli. He is listed as Pasquale Brelli, the O in his last name omitted.

(c. 2001)

The Old Oak Tree

Twenty-two years ago when we moved into our present house there was but one tree on the property, a mature beech in the far right corner. On the empty lot next to us was but one tree also: a huge, towering oak.

When Ken and Yvonne Yockel and their three kids moved in next door a year later, they planted trees with the same kind of abandon we had. Our corner of the former corn field became heavily treed indeed.

But when the Yockel kids, Sue, Tammy and Kurt and our three sought refuge from the summer heat, or looked for a special place to picnic or pitch a tent, it was under the old oak, its shade far superior to anything the newer plantings had to offer.

Over the years as our children and those next door grew and eventually left home, the old oak showed signs of dying, one huge limb after the other failing to leaf out in spring.

Still the old oak was not lonely. Rabbits scampered underneath. Squirrels ran up and down its mighty trunk and its bare limbs. Crows perched in the uppermost skeletal fingers, silhouetted against the sky, their silent blackness more menacing than any sound to those who allowed their imaginations free rein.

"There was always an uneven number, usually five," Yvonne said, her comment causing a delicious thrill in those who looked at the tree and saw Poe not Penfield.

Now and then Ken talked about having the oak taken down, but as the years passed and the tree remained, we thought perhaps it might outlast us all.

Then two weeks ago from inside I heard buzz saws. High in the oak's branches was a young man armed with a power saw. Two more men were on the ground, one an experienced hand who directed where the cuts should be made, what angle, where precisely the first huge limbs would fall.

I watched as the first heavy limbs came down with a roar and a thump that shook the ground and tore at the heart.

"Rotten," said Ken. "We were afraid we'd be at the lake and get word it had been hit by lightning and done all kinds of damage."

"Ants," said the knowledgeable expert.

"How old?" I asked later in the day as the mighty trunk, at least four feet in diameter, lay on its side.

"Hard to tell," thanks to rot obliterating part of the identifying circles. But when pressed, the guess was 150 years plus.

The stones in the graveyard across from our tract date back to then and I wondered about the Indians and settlers who had sought shelter under the broad protective arms of that encompassing oak. And I thought of our kids who had shared in the last decades of the old oak's life and in whose memories it will never fall.

(c. 1995)

April Discovery

It all began with an innocuous e-mail to my four siblings with a special message to Paul, the youngest, who happens to own an SUV and lives in McKean County, Pa. He'd promised to help search for our great-grandparents' homestead in neighboring North Central Potter County. Our great-grandparents had settled a stone's throw from the tiny depot of the logging railroad which had hired my great-grandfather. Now there were only a couple of shed-size buildings that had been converted to hunting and fishing camps. I'd been there in September, but lack of time and fear of rattlers drove me out.

Sister Thomasina who lives in Rockland County outside NYC picked up on my message and announced electronically she wanted to join us. We set a date, the first Wednesday of April, but a forecast for the thirties caused us to reset it for the following week. The forecast was for even chillier weather. I emailed Paul and said I'd leave exploring until later in the year.

"Oh, no you're not. We're going," was the response. And go we did along with Thom's husband Ted and Paul's Maggie, 5, who was just getting over a strep infection.

We set out before 10 a.m. with a lunch that Paul packed: sandwich fixings, fruit and a surprise—a jug of Zinfandel—a wine not unlike pink lemonade. Not the beverage of choice when the wind chill is 15. (The strongest thing Paul imbibes is Coke on the rocks.)

With only one pit stop on our way, we arrived at the entrance just north of Wharton to the abandoned railroad bed which led to Hammersley Junction.. The road was soggy with missing chunks of packed clay, thanks to rivulets cascading down the mountain side. We came to a grassy field, parked, knowing the rest of the trip would be by foot.

"I'm hungry," said Maggie. A chorus of "Me, toos," prompted Paul to open the tailgate and we dug in. Changing from a light jacket to a heavy, hooded coat plus fleece hat, I eyed the one beverage and wished loudly for hot coffee. "That was your responsibility," said my hard-hearted sibling. "You should have packed a thermos." Little brother, as you might have guessed, doesn't drink coffee, either.

It was time to get into the spirit of the day and stop grousing over the wind chill. Winter picnics, a tradition in our family, can be the most fun, if the most challenging.

I started building a sandwich-turkey, cheese, whole wheat bread and some kind of delicious mustard with horse radish. Thom and Ted were drinking the Zinfandel from small paper cups as protection against the cold. I followed suit. Thanks to the company, the elements and the sense of adventure, the repast including the "lemonade" was ambrosial.

It was time for the adventure. The railroad bed had disappeared but by skirting a half acre of water, we were soon on the trail again. "Just a little less than a mile ahead," I told the crew. We walked a mile and half north and then retraced our steps. No place on the steep mountain side where a house and barn could have been located. Maggie, up to now, a real trouper, wanted to be carried. Her two aunts grabbed her little hands and swung her high over more rivulets. The distraction did the trick and eventually we were back to the SUV. There we realized the only spot where the homestead could have been was on a slope we'd passed earlier very near where we'd parked. A family photo from the early 1900 shows the farm adjacent to a tiny depot, a junction of the Buffalo and Susquehanna Railway and the logging tram tracks that brought the timber over the mountain shortly after the turn of the century.

This had been my fourth research trip (for *Growing Up Italian in God's Country*) and a fine sense of history reigned. We celebrated with what else?—more Zinfandel and potato chips. Back at Paul's house, Brother Sam who wasn't able to join us, but has often explored the area in his dune buggy, promised to go with me when the weather was more suitable. Oh, yes.

(c. 1999)

Riley Turns Four

The three-year-old turns four today, May 2. Happy Birthday, Riley James Bartlett. Last week the two of us had a pre-celebration.. Older brother Austin, 7, was at school, and Quinn, 2 at the end of the month, cooperated by taking a two-hour nap for the sitter.

"Where do we eat?" I asked. His choice: a Happy Meal, with chicken nuggets, Fwench Fwies and chocolate shake. A verbal child, he did not eat much, busy as he was with commenting on everyone and everything in sight and trying to make the plastic toy work. He also did his best to give me a play-by-play on the family's previous week in Disney World. "They didn't have strawberry jelly at Disney World, only grape for the peanut butter sandwich. I like grape now. Do you have any grape jelly?" (Two weeks ago he wouldn't touch it.) "I need to go to the bathroom." We go.

Back at our house, I discover we need to make an emergency trip to the grocery store. I strap him in and we start. Riley's spatial intelligence kicks in. "I didn't know the playground was this close to your house. Let's go to the playground."

"Afterward, "I mumble. "Now," he says. "After," I repeat, but his attention is already elsewhere. "Look at that school bus. A little one. When I was little," he says, " I used to call them baby buses." He laughs at his previous childish ways.

At the grocery we need quarters, lots of quarters, for the one -armed bandits they put in the front of the store to dispense treacherous plastic miniature toys that his two-year-old brother will put in his mouth. "I'll hide it from Quinn," he says. I lose that battle, plus the one for a small bottle of apple juice. At the free cookie section, he takes three. "One for me, one for Quinn, one for Austin." I wrap them in wax paper and quickly stuff them in his pocket. Since his parents spend a couple of hundred dollars a week at that establishment, I figure the store can absorb the cost of two extra free cookies. On the way back we pass the playground again. "Now," he says. I agree that we'll drop off the stuff we bought and come right back, which we do.

"Look," Riley says. "There's the library. If we have to go to the bathroom we can go there." Very good, I say. He runs for the bouncy frog and climbs on it. "Ribbit, Ribbit." From there it's to the swings. "Push me, Namah." I push. " I have to go to the bathroom." I remind him that he just went to the bathroom. "I have to go again." We walk to the library. After 15 minutes I start pleading to go home. "No." I tell him we have to pick up pinecones in the back yard.

"No. Oh, okay." We go home and head for the back yard. We pick up pinecones. I find the shovel. The dog has been busy. Riley is delighted. "Here, Namah. Poop, poop, poop. Here and here and here!" After

a while I tell him it might be time to watch "Scooby Doo and the Alien Invaders". This works almost every time. Not today.

"First," Riley says, "we go to the basement and play ping pong." I tell him I need a rest. "I don't," he says. "Ping Pong, Namah. Now. In the basement." He uses the peremptory tone he has learned from his older sibling and cousin.

All right, I concede, but I stick in the video and tell him I have to relax for just a minute since our pingpong games consist mostly of my picking up balls off the floor. I take one end of the couch and he takes the other. It looks as if his eyelids might be lowering. I close mine and send up a prayer. I open one eye. Yes! His are closed. I carefully remove his glasses and study the sweet face, then quickly lie back to gird for the next round of activities. Riley sleeps for 20 minutes, then sits upright. "Pingpong, Namah" he says. "Now!

(2001)

Memories

I have been filling out memory books for my daughters. Starting two years ago last Mother's Day, I am still at it. The version incudes stories about my mother, their grandmother; my own growing-up days and theirs. Some sections are difficult to complete, e.g., "What did I learn from you, my daugher?" One misstep and it becomes sloppily sentimental. Go in the other direction, and your words sound distant and cool.

I was stuck for a long time on the page which asks for my favorite "words". Perhaps the author meant for me to include a poem. Not into poetry, I think, then remember the best.

They that hope in the Lord will renew their strength, they will soar as with eagles' wings;

They will run and not grow weary, walk and not grow faint. (Isaiah 40:31)

One particular section was a breeze to fill out, a favorite recipe, one we all love. No contest. The hands-down winner is:

BLACKBERRY PIE

DIRECTIONS: jump in the car and go to Potter or McKean County in Pennsylvania, land where our family has been berrying since 1890s. Climb a mountain where timber has been slashed. Find new growth, specifically blackberry brambles.

Wear long pants and a long-sleeved shirt. You'll still get scratches but the expedition won't be the same without them.

Take along a silver lard pail with handle so you can hear the berries "ping" as they hit the bottom.

Pick some, eat some. Watch out for bears while you do. They enjoy blackberries, too.

Pick out and throw away twigs and green berries from your pail. Eat some more.

Take time for a picnic. Find a mountain spring with cold, sweet water so chilly and delicious it will make your teeth ache.

Brush off any tiny bugs on

the back of your neck and throat. Pick some more.

Breathe in clean, clear air, the scent of the woods, old leaves, decaying logs, mushrooms and moss. Have a few more berries, choose the biggest and juiciest.

Head for home. If there are any berries left, make a pie.

(c. 2000)

Why Rochester?

Many years ago when our children were small, the late legendary newsman and outdoorsman Floyd King and his second wife, Agnes, invited us all for supper at their home backing up to Ellison Park in Penfield. It was a delightful evening, Floyd being an old friend and co-worker on the Democrat and Chronicle.

My husband and Floyd worked together as copy editors at one end of the city room. I had left the morning newspaper to raise our family some time before, but I recall well being summoned to the horseshoe desk to explain a word, a fact, an attribution I'd used in a story, and later, in my daily TV column.

There was little newspaper talk that evening. Instead Floyd and the plainspoken Agnes, a match for her husband in aims, attitude and love of nature, toured their grounds with us showing us their extensive garden, explaining the virtues of the Jerusalem artichoke,

serving us boiled chestnuts from a tree in their yard. There was also an invitation to visit their farm south of Rochester which we took them up on. In retrospect I realized they were not only environmentalists and conservationists, but avid teachers.

Floyd was my husband's friend, but he and I also had a bond as transplanted Pennsylvanians, Floyd being from Warren, I from neighboring McKean County. Just recently I came across a yellowed, treasured column he'd written on the Mountain Laurel that grows in our beloved Allegheny mountains. And I remembered that he sometimes asked us to bring him back some scrapple when we visited my folks.

But it was Agnes King who was to make a lasting impression on me. The first time we met her, Floyd explained just how Agnes, who had lived in the mid-west, decided to come to western New York State. She took out a map of the United

States and studied it closely, then chose Rochester.

"Why?" asked Floyd rhetorically. "Because there were no floods, tornadoes, hurricanes or other such natural hazards to worry about.

Watching the pictures of the devastation in Florida this past weekend, I thought of again of this intrepid woman and lifted my morning cup in salute. "Smart move, Agnes. Right on."

(c. 2003)

Five Weeks Later: After the Twin Towers

I tell my husband, a member of the media, to be careful opening mail. (He says a policy has been in place from the beginning to discard letters with no return address.)

I call my older daughter who works on the 21st floor of a downtown building to remind her to be aware. (She says an emergency drill has been scheduled for that morning.)

I warn my younger daughter who is in and out of New York City on a regular basis to avoid tunnels, stay off the bridges at rush hour and avoid crowds. Ha! (Done, she says).

I hear from a friend who long ago moved to Washington. We are fine, she says, but her office window overlooks the capitol—making for interesting days in the face of unconfirmed reports, rumors etc.

I quiz the oldest grandchild carefully. Have they been discussing the events of Sept.

11 in class? No, he says and I wonder who is shielding whom.

I stop in a department store halfway home from Pennsylvania and hear two clerks talking. One says she is against war, but in this case… Back in the car I turn on the radio and learn that the bombing has begun.

At home I turn on the TV and go from one news channel to another. Turn off the TV, my kids say. You need to get away from it.

I wake in the middle of the night from a bad dream, quieting the panic inside by invoking the paraclete.

We go to church. It is the right place to be. The choirmaster has chosen a Quaker hymn, "How Can I Keep from Singing." I love the melody, pay scant attention to the words until the third stanza which begins "When tyrants tremble sick with fear— and hear their death knells ringing…" and I pray, "Oh, yes, God, please." *(2001)*

"You Can Go Home Again."

A recent email from a friend in Potter County, Pa. sent me into a delightful tizzy. He'd recently spoken with the owners of my grandparents' former home. They'd obtained a copy of, "Growing Up Italian in God's Country", and wanted to meet me. I made contact via their daughter and boldly suggested we meet at their place, a camp for these last 60 years. There was an ulterior motive. I hoped upon hope they would invite me inside the old house which held such dear memories.

A date was agreed upon and knowing how much it would please my two aunts, both of whom were born there, I called them at the last minute asking them to come. The hope was that the owners would realize just how much this meant to us, especially Louise and Madeline, my mother's younger sisters.

I started out from Rochester on a rainy Saturday morning.

By noon as I reached Potter County and Conrad, once a bustling logging town, sunshine had transformed the familiar mountainous landscape.

On the outside the house built by my grandfather has changed very little over the years. A modest frame structure covered in green shingles, it is situated a few feet alongside a stream known as the East Fork of the Sinnemahoning. Grandpa took my grandmother there as a bride in 1915, moving her 7 miles north from her home in Hammersley Junction, a logging terminus.

My grandfather, Patsy Borelli, a foreman first on The Buffalo and Susquehanna, and later on the Baltimore and Ohio when it bought out the logging railroad, had built the homestead right below the tracks that ran on the side of the mountain above the creek. In summer of 1942 a flood that devastated Potter

County tore up the B&O tracks below Conrad necessitating his transfer.

In a book now in progress, my uncle Al describes how stoic my grandfather was as their furnishings were placed on a railroad car and taken to West Pike, a hamlet near Galeton. But as he drove over the wooden bridge crossing the stream, Grandpa looked back for the last time and broke down. "Goodbye old house, you have been good to us," were his parting words.

I arrived at the house before noon to find both aunts and their husbands there in the dining room with our hosts, Joanne and Bob Waltersdorff from York, Pa. On the dining room table was a stack of books waiting to be signed, one for the Waltersdorffs and for each of their five children.

Madeline had already wiped tears from her eyes as she had eyed the path my grandfather had taken each morning from home to the tiny RRstation above. Inside we noted the changes that had been made over the years. A third window had been cut in the west wall to take advantage of the picturesque stream. An alcove in the dining room had been enlarged and one of two front doors eliminated.

Most radical were electric lights and appliances. A room off the kitchen once housing Gram's generator-powered washing machine was now a bathroom, the outdoor two-seater demoted. With glee we noted that the linoleum on the kitchen floor, a red and black design, was the original. Ditto for the linoleum upstairs.

I crept into the back bedroom which Madeline and Louise had shared and where we grandchildren often slept when visiting. There was the remembered sloping ceiling, the sprigged wallpaper giving way to paneling. We ran hands over the original doors, jiggling the antiquated key boxes.

But it was in my grandparents' former bedroom that the memories came flooding in. It was there my mother Margaret was born in 1917—indeed where all Gram's babies were born, including, Paul and Helena, who died in infancy. Through an open window I could hear the babble of the stream which had once lulled us to sleep along with the haunting song of the whippoorwill perched in the nearby hemlock. It was here too that I awoke with croup unable to breathe. My grandfather wrapped me in his sheepskin coat and took me outside until the moist night air filled my lungs. In the kitchen Gram poured a noxious mixture of Vicks and melted butter down my throat to keep it open.

Back downstairs, the Waltersdorffs added to their warm and gracious welcome, offering us a large framed picture of the house and stream. But there was another even more precious gift: The original deed to the house, signed by my grandparents, brought the tears I'd so far avoided.

The get-together ended with hugs, photos and many thanks on our part.

All the way home I thought of the heartache wrapped up in the official document I had greedily seized. Easing that memory was another: one of the family picture Joanne Waltersdorff showed me. Knowing her and Bob's children and grandchildren, all of whom had enjoyed the house, the land and stream as our family once had, was balm to a full heart.

Note: My uncle Alfred Borelli's book, "The East Fork Revisited: A Memoir," is now in print.

(c. 2004)

The Price of War

A much loved friend from another part of the country e-mails me. She forwards a letter from an U.S. Army officer in Iraq, a graduate of West Point. His purpose is to tell the American people that despite what we hear via the media, things are going swimmingly in Iraq. Schools are being built, government is being established, rebuilding of infrastructure under way.

Because this friend is very dear to me, I do not respond as I'd like to. I do not, because I respect her, and because friendship is more important to me than arguing politics. But the email stays with me and so I take this route.

To wit: I, too, have the greatest admiration and deepest gratitude for our American military men and women. And I hope to get a chance to cast a presidential vote for one who was first in his class at West Point. If not the Five Star General, then the Senator who earned a Silver Star, Bronze Star and three Purple Hearts during his stint in the Navy fighting the Viet Nam war. As both candidates have indicated, anyone who has actually fought a war knows the terrible price that is paid by those who fight it. Thus, the idea of a preemptive war is anathema. The idea of starting a preemptive war, based on skewed half truths, is criminal.

As I write this, 501 U.S. military men and women have been killed in Iraq. We are told that not all the lives were lost in combat, some were in accidents and other non-combat deaths. The distinction escapes me.

Try to estimate the number of people affected by one soldier's death, some of whom will feel the loss for the rest of their lives. Is it 25? 50? 100? 500? 1000? Or more? (In the series of small towns I grew up in, a resident lost is a neighbor mourned by all 2000.)

Think of the anguish of parents, siblings, grandparents, friends and extended family.

Forget for a moment, if we can, the dead we have lost. Think of the number of wounded. Young men and women losing feet, legs, hands, arms, eyes. Lives forever changed. How many? Back in August one newspaper estimated the unofficial number was in the thousands, many times the actual number reported. How many more in the 4-1/2 months since then we can only guess. The tally of maimed U.S. soldiers is kept under wraps.

I leave until last the innocent Iraqi civilians. Untold thousands have paid with their lives. The counter argument is that many more lives were lost under the former regime. Is not the point of liberation to protect the citizens from more bloodshed?

By writing the above, I leave myself open to the charge of being a Bush hater. Not true. What I hate is war. Most particularly war which may expose our land and our people to more fear and bloodshed than we have already experienced, create even more chaos and unrest in the Middle East, and turn the rest of the world against us for decades to come.

(2004)

Where Your Treasure Is

On the way into church last week something caught my eye. In a side vestibule displayed prominently on a rack of reading material was a small pamphlet. Can't remember the exact title but the fact that it had something to do with voting made me pick it up. I read a few lines which exhorted fellow Catholics to **vote the right way.** *It doesn't matter if the candidate stumbles and can't produce a coherent sentence. The only important quality is that he is pro-life, it read.* I stuck the pamphlet behind the other booklets, then thought better of it, and returned it to its prominent spot. Most of the Catholics I know are an independent lot and would resent being told how to vote.

Besides I'd already been dealing with this kind of reasoning closer to home. Of my four siblings only one agrees with me on who should be making life and death decisions in the White House.

Years ago when things weren't as inflammatory as they are in this election season, I was lectured on the sanctity of life, meaning the unborn. I agreed, with exceptions for rape and the health of the mother, but then posed the question about the death penalty for criminals.

"Oh, but they're not innocent," came the reply. (Never mind that dozens on death row have been found to be so.) My larger point was that the Christian teaching (which they were invoking and which I understood the Catholic bishops to uphold) was that all life was sacred.

This includes the nearly 1100 Americans who have perished since the U.S. declared war in the middle east and the countless thousands of Iraqi citizens.

But my dissenting family members have another, perhaps more pressing, argument. I should be more business-like, one emails me. "Had Bush's tax credits been in effect when our father died, we'd have received more money."

I email back that there are more important things to consider, i.e. the very real possibility of my grandsons being drafted and sent to war versus a tax credit. I also send a quote from Matthew, "Remember where your treasure is, there your heart is also." I fail to point out that under Clinton our stock was worth twice what it is now. But the damage is done nonetheless. My sibling emails me back that unless I cease and desist, invitations to visit will be withdrawn.

Eventually we all take an electronic vow to not discuss politics. Our familial bond is more important than our conflicting views.

I suspect that ours is not the only family to be torn apart in this election season. My hope is that after Nov. 2, we and a nation will reconcile.

(2004)

Most Memorable Election

The election of 2004, the most intense I can remember, is over. Whether we will have a clear winner by the time you read this is another matter. As exhilarating as it has been to see so many people engaged, it was not the most exciting election I can remember. That distinction goes to 1960, one in which I played a small part reporting on campaign visits to Rochester.

I had come the year before to the Democrat and Chronicle from a small daily in Pennsylvania where I'd been "women's page editor" dealing with weddings and other frivolities. Yearning to cover news, I got my wish, and then some, as one of two female general assignment reporters. Happily for me, the other woman, my good friend Jean Utter, had Thursdays off. It so happened that was the day on successive weeks in October that the candidates visited.

Almost before I realized what was happening I was sitting in the back seat of a convertible with Lady Bird Johnson on the trip from the airport to headquarters at the old Manger Hotel, now Midtown Plaza. I was impressed with her warmth, humor and intelligence as she told me something about their daughters, how she had met Lyndon, and the rigors of the campaign trail. Ethel Kennedy, standing in for her pregnant sister-in-law Jackie Kennedy, was comparatively reserved at a later interview that day.

That evening I stole my way to within a few feet of JFK in the Manger ballroom where he was holding forth, but because of the crush and my lack of height, I couldn't actually see him. Jean Walrath, D&C theater editor assured me, however, that he was "delicious" looking.

The wife of Henry Cabot Lodge, Nixon's V.P. candidate, was vivacious and outgoing on a bus ride from the airport on another occasion, but Pat Nixon was not available to the press. I had to be content with sitting in the front row and jotting down her embarrassed reactions as her husband spoke to a packed War Memorial.

Perhaps the most memorable moment during those visits was when I met India Edwards, DNC executive, at the Manger. She pulled me into a vacant hotel room on the second floor to escape the noise and crush of reporters from around the country who were jamming the hallways. We pulled up two chairs and, notebook in hand, I began asking questions.

Then an inner door opened and Mrs. Edwards gasped as a man walked out of the bathroom. She urged me to my feet, but Lyndon Johnson waved an expansive hand. "No need to leave, ladies." We scurried out, nevertheless, to be greeted by local and national reporters wondering how we'd gained access to the private room of the man who would become vice president a few weeks later, and in one of the most tragic days in this country's history, ascend to the presidency.

(c. 2004)

Spaghetti Sauces
I Have Known

A culinary truism: There are as many tomato sauces as there are Italian cooks. The one we cook at our house is different from what my mother made. Mom's was different than that produced by both grandmothers. All were distinctive and delicious. I loved them all, including that of my Irish mother-in-law, the former Helen Fitzgerald. She was taught by her mother-in-law, my husband's Italian grandma, Carmela, and who, his mother thought, might just have left out an ingredient or two.

In addition to the tomato base, all recipes, however, had one thing in common. They were as easy to make as they were delicious to eat.

Thus, I am always astounded by the number of people who buy jars of sauce off the shelf. Some time ago the head of the house, forewarned that I didn't feel like cooking, came home with a glass container of the stuff. I cooked some shells or maybe it was penne, warmed up the contents of the jar, and poured it on the cooked pasta. It was, if you'll excuse the phrase, "god-awful".

At my next opportunity, I went to the store and began examining the label contents of several brands. Even Paul Newman's much vaunted brand began with the same ingredient: Crushed tomatoes, made from!!!! tomato paste and water. Uggh. That was not the worst of it. The next ingredient in Newman's Own and many other canned sauces turned out to be that famous Italian ingredient: corn syrup! The manufacturers who are so clever coming up with Italian names for their products then add some soybean oil and follow it with?

What else, but high fructose

corn syrup!!! To compensate for all the cheap ingredients they add heavy doses of dried herbs, and of course, chemicals to retard spoilage. I can just imagine my little grandmothers and their mothers and grandmothers turning over in their graves.

Years ago on one of our first trips to Italy, my husband and I were thrilled with the light sauces served on our pasta. No all day simmering which can turn tomatoes so dark they look almost black. Ever since that trip, we simmer sauce for 45 minutes at the most. If you know an Italian grandmother, ask her how to make it. If not, here's how my husband and I make it.

Brown skinned chicken thighs or Italian style poultry sausage in a little extra virgin olive oil. Add a 39-ounce can of good quality crushed tomatoes, a couple cloves of garlic minced and a few leaves of fresh basil. (I keep a container of it growing in front of the sliding glass door.) Heat until just below boiling. Reduce heat and simmer for 45 minutes. This will top 1 pound of spaghetti or macaroni. Serve and add grated Pecorino Romano or Parmesan.

If you prefer meatless sauce, saute until translucent, but do not brown, several cloves of garlic in a 1/3 cup of extra virgin olive oil. Remove garlic, add crushed tomatoes, more minced garlic and a few leaves of fresh basil. Continue as above. Enjoy!

(Note: The head of the house always adds more olive oil to the pot than I do. You can also double or triple the above amounts and use it during the week as daughter-in-law Victoria does.

Fat Is Not
A 4-Letter Word

Our older daughter's birthday was coming up and the gang voted to celebrate it on the actual day, the 15ᵗʰ. "That's the first Friday of Lent," I reminded them. "No meat."

Lasagna would do fine, they agreed, and so last Friday I set to work gathering the ingredients and putting the pasta dish together, plus a vegetable melange, and Johanna's favorite chocolate cake. A trip to the nearby Sicilian bakery, Bel Vedere, for two loaves of dense, deliciously crusty bread was also on the agenda.

That night our children (the 6 grandchildren still prefer white pasta with butter on it) all raved about the lasagna. What was different? I confessed that in my haste to shop, I'd inadvertently grabbed a carton of whole milk ricotta—verboten in our house devoted to heart-healthy cooking for the past 20 years. True, I'd blended the whole milk product with another carton of part skim milk ricotta. Still the difference was noticeable. Just possibly a lapse on special occasions is not out of line.

As the grand chefs remind us on the TV cooking shows, nothing tastes as good as fat. Unless it is fat and sugar. Which is why the birthday girl had requested chocolate frosting made with butter—none of that white shortening that goes in commercial bakery frosting.

Taste is also why I did not skimp on the extra virgin olive oil (the healthiest of fats) in sautéing garlic for the marinara sauce. Ditto for the ratatouille, a vegetable stew introduced into our repertoire some years ago by my sister Jude. Whatever its origin(French or Italian), it is delicious and the fastest way to get the vegetable dodgers to eat their daily five. Zucchini, eggplant, red and green peppers, mushrooms and onions are cut into one-inch chunks and sauteed in, what else, extra virgin oil. Some cooks are depraved enough to top it with shredded mozzarella and put it the oven or microwave for a moment until the cheese is melted. Not I. At least not this time. Just the merest sprinkling of Pecorino Romano. Equally good hot or cold, the leftovers make a great midnight snack. After all, you can't eat too many vegetables.

(c. 2003)

The Visitor

When we moved to our new home some 30 years ago, there was one tree on our suburban plot. Desiring to simulate the rural Pennsylvania setting I'd grown up in and missed sorely, we planted and planted on our 2/3 acre. If I couldn't have mountains, I'd at least have trees. True to fashion, we overdid it, a fact we are very much aware of at leaf-raking time.

On the other hand we seldom have to turn on the air conditioner until after noon on the steamiest days thanks to the shade of the three huge sycamores. But that was not the best thing about our contrived woodland. Wildlife was attracted to our pie-shaped refuge. Flocks of pheasants once could be seen most mornings strutting, under the row of honeysuckle bushes to the north. A new tract replacing a nearby meadow put a stop to that. Cardinals, blue-jays, red-head woodpeckers and mourning doves are among those whose calls still enliven the back yard while humming-birds sip from red petunias. And once the cover is off and before the chlorine treatment begins, mallards take over the water, sunning themselves at poolside.

There were also larger visitors. Some years ago we awoke one snowy January morning to find several deer rounding our pool fence. Most impressive was a buck whose antlered rack equaled Bambi's father's and then some. More recently parties of does use the east border of the yard to cross from one nearby wooded area to another. This in spite of the presence of Luke Skywalker who roams the back yard barking furiously at tree-hopping squirrels and audacious chipmunks.

This past Sunday morning I changed clothes and began to transfer dirt from a crumbling half barrel on the front stoop to a new container still smelling of Jack Daniels. Out back my husband began cleaning the pool. Preparatory to putting in the red and pink geraniums,

I started around the side of the house to get a trowel and stopped in my tracks.

There nestled up against the basement window behind the miniature rose bush was a tiny fawn, two weeks old at the most. It gazed up at me, no fear in the serene brown eyes. I scanned the neighboring thicket hoping to glimpse the mother. No sign or movement. Alerting my husband not to let the dog out, I went back to my geraniums, checking every so often to see if the fawn was still there. Unconcerned it had curled itself up in Luke fashion, its head resting on its front paws, and was napping.

Clouds were now overhead with a forecast of heavy showers. The fawn hadn't moved. The roof overhang gave scant protection. After some argument with my city-bred husband, I called animal control. The best thing to do, I was assured, was to wait for the mother to make her move. Torn between wanting to cover the rosebush to afford the baby some protection and letting nature take its course, I chose the latter. Good time to run an errand. But I'd no sooner driven away than the rain came in earnest and by the time I'd reached the plaza it was so heavy I berated myself for not having done something, anything to afford the beautiful spotted baby some shelter. Obviously it would not move until signaled to do so.

Returning, I went immediately into the garage to find a large piece of cardboard which when placed on top of the bush might help a little. I crept around the side of the house to find… nothing. The rain and deserted yard had done the trick. With a huge sense of relief I sent up thanks for the encounter with one of His most beautiful creatures on this Sabbath day.

(2004)

Discovering Our Roman Roots In U.K.

Abruptly, and to my amazement, we changed travel plans. Thanks to the whim of a young grandson, our proposed journey to Italy, the latest in a long series, would become instead a trip to England. But as we would discover, we were never far in the U.K. from our ancestral roots, particularly those of my Roman grandfather.

Our trip to England began this way: " How would you like to go with us to Rome and Pompeii?" I asked A.J., 12, envisioning seeing the Colosseum and Vesuvius through a youngster's eyes once again.

"I wouldn't," said the oldest of our seven grandchildren. "I'd rather go to London."

"To London?"

"To see Big Ben and the other landmarks."

"*Why not go to England*?" my husband asked upon hearing A.J.'s response . "We could fly into London and take a train north to spend a couple of days with Lina and her family."

Years ago while on vacation near Sorrento, my husband Carmen and I sought out his family's native village of Bellona near Naples, which his father long ago turned his back on.

We discovered a family who shared his last name plus a great-grandfather in common. Some months later, my husband received a letter from one Lina Pancaro, a young woman in Cheshire. Lina's parents had emigrated from Bellona to England to seek work in the 1950s. She'd just returned from a visit to Bellona and learned of her American cousin. Soon Lina and my husband were corresponding, she eventually visiting us twice in our Rochester suburb.

Lina frequently encouraged us to come to their small town in Cheshire to meet the rest of her family. From what we had gathered from her visits and letters, they lived very much in the spirit of their forebears, speaking Italian to each other, intertwining English and Italian cuisines and traveling regularly back to Bellona to see relatives.

"Come," said Lina eagerly when I made that first call. She suggested we fly into Manchester and use her home outside the industrial center as a base for our travels. "It's only 2 1/2 hours to London by express train," she pointed out "and a thirty minute flight to Dublin." Beautiful Derbyshire and the Peak District are next door and Scotland and Hadrian's Wall (my main objective) a two-hour drive north. Wales, to the south, is even closer.

Thus it was on the promise of enjoying new vistas and connecting with Italian family that we bought tickets and headed for Manchester on A.J.'s last day of school.

Certain doubts plagued us on the flight, as indeed they had at each stage of our preparations e.g., What were we doing heading for a climate rainier and chillier than our own? And while the previous winter had dumped less snow on Rochester than usual, the gloom and dampness had taken its toll in aching joints and drooping spirits. But it was

summer and hadn't Shakespeare extolled the rare day in June. As it turned out, early summer warmth in Cheshire was rare indeed. Happily, we had heeded Lina's advice to pack clothes that could be layered. But the warmth of the Italian-English welcome balanced any weather complaints and then some.

Our 6:30 a.m. arrival in Manchester gave us an indication of what lay ahead. There waiting for us was Lina, her sister Antonietta (Toni) and brother-in-law Raffaele (Raff). They had brought two cars, fearful our luggage would not fit in just one of the compact Fords.

The drive to Hyde, once a thriving textile center, southeast of Manchester, took about twenty minutes. After allowing us a brief rest, the warm welcome continued with a "full English breakfast" of eggs, sausages, grilled tomatoes and baked beans at Lina's home followed by a larger get-together that night where we met her brother Peter and assorted other relatives.

The next day after Mass at St. Paul's Roman Catholic Church, where Lina, her brother and sister are all eucharistic ministers, we were invited to her sister's for Sunday "lunch".

The World Cup was on the Telly and one after another of the men in the family showed up wearing Italia soccer shirts, clearly indicating where their loyalties lay when it came to "football".

Expecting a light meal, we were served lasagna and bracciole, salads, bread, fruit and sweets with the wine flowing throughout. Four of their six grown children showed up plus two grandchildren, and in-laws.

It was a scenario repeated again and again. Rosanna, who had visited us in the U.S. on Lina's last trip invited us to a Saturday night get-together at her home in Gee Cross. Her late mother was Italian-born as was her Aunt Esterina who brought homemade red wine. At times we seemed to do more eating than anything else. Espresso was brewed at the end of every meal, as a pick-me-up any time of the day and at every drop-in visit. Each time an accompanying sweet was offered, reminding us that the Italian biscotti and the English biscuit have the same root.

Worry about calories quickly dissipated as nearly every repast was followed by "Are you ready for a walk?" The Italian *passegiata* was much in vogue

with the family. Following Sunday lunch, the men headed up to the park at Werneth Low, the highest spot in the town from which one could see adjacent Derbyshire. Meanwhile the women all walked back to church for the annual flower show with tea and scones served in the garden. The return walk was interrupted by a stop at a nephew's trendy condo where espresso was quickly brewed.

The fear we'd not be able to explore farther afield was groundless. In fact Lina accompanied us to Dublin and London for a couple of days stay each, obtaining excellent rates and helping us negotiate unfamiliar territory.

The first group foray was to Buxton, a spa and resort town where Lina's parents had first settled upon arrival from Italy in 1950. By chance, they had chosen as their first home in the U.K., a site established by the Romans nearly two thousand years before. The Spa's first name: *Aquae Armentiae*. After an extended walk around the hill-top town, and lunch at an old English pub where the offerings included a surprisingly good lasagna, it was on to neighboring Chatsworth. The grand estate of the Duke and Duchess of Devonshire is open to the public for a price including, for an extra fee, entrance into the suite occupied by Mary Queen of Scots who stayed there more than once as a "captive" guest.

Ten of us went together to Lyme Hall, not far from Hyde, an estate now under the auspices of the National Trust. It was a place I had particularly wanted to see, its exterior one of those used for the filming of the 1995 production of "Pride and Prejudice." And if I was subconsciously hoping to see Darcy striding across the grounds and gardens of "Pemberley", a school orchestra in the inner courtyard compensated with show tunes, prompting Lina's sister-in-law Christine, to do a sprightly, if modest, "Can Can" in the rain.

A.J., meanwhile, found a family companion in Eliot, also 12. At Chatsworth, A.J. toured the public rooms with the rest of us, but was more interested in the elaborate maze on magnificent grounds that sported stream, lake and falls. At Lyme Hall he and Eliot amused themselves by hiding in the bushes, springing out to surprise the adults who were searching for them.

In Ireland, my husband celebrated his mother's Fitzgerald roots and for two days the Italian culture gave way to things Irish including a quick visit to the Book of Kells at Trinity College and later the Writer's Museum paying tribute to Joyce, Shaw, Swift, Yeats among others. Happily the tour bus guide's bawdy allusions to Oscar Wilde passed over our grandson's head. We drank tea and coffee latte at Bewley's café, around the corner from our Temple Bar Hotel in the city's cultural and entertainment district, and stout at the Guiness Storehouse, while promising ourselves another longer visit to Ireland.

But for the rest of the trip we were never far from being reminded of the Roman influence, both past and present. Manchester, site of Roman fortifications and London, the town which had started it all, offered not only archeological excavations ruins, but the London tour guide noted that the city's location had been chosen by the Romans as the best place to cross the Thames. At the British Museum, we moved from the Rosetta Stone and the Elgin Marbles to a room given over to Magna Graecia, my paternal grandparents' stomping grounds.

The indefatigable Lina marched us through Covent

Garden, Hyde Park and Harrods, where. A.J. purchased souvenir mugs for his parents, and a thick paperback book for himself. To please our grandson, we ate pizza at Italian restaurants twice, although Lina noted that the staff in the Kensington eatery was speaking Spanish to one another. We fared better at Zia Teresa's in Knightsbridge.

It was small, picturesque Hyde, however, with its terrace homes and public buildings dating as far back as the 1700s, surrounded by gently rolling hills and boasting a Roman road on which we had traveled to Buxton, that made an indelible impression. For Hyde, like Robert Louis Stevenson's eponymous character, had another side.

On one of our first walks to the open air market, Lina pointed out Dr. Harold Shipman's surgery at 22 Market Street. At that point the family doctor had been accused of killing 15 of his patients. By the time our visit had ended, the number of victims had gone up to 215 with another 45 where there were "real suspicions" and a further 38 possibles. Shipman is now described as Britain's worst mass murderer.

"We knew something was wrong," Lina's sister said. "One of his victims was a eucharistic minister at our church. She was distributing communion one Sunday morning and the next day she was dead." Shipman's lethal injections were made at both his surgery and during impromptu housecalls.

These were not the first murders to make their town infamous. In the late 1960s a string of child abductions and grisly killings by Hyde residents became known as the Moor Murders.

If these chilling realities cast a pall, it was offset by the relatives' affability. As we surveyed the mountain of gifts — from Wimbledon towels made by Raff's firm, books, lace tablecloth, an espresso coffee pot, a World Cup "football" and shirt for A.J.— we eyed our luggage. Lina again came to the rescue with a suitcase twice as large as any of ours to carry home our Italian/English gifts .

Ironically we didn't get to Hadrian's Wall, the barrier erected 2000 years ago by Roman soldiers to keep the Picts from the north from invading Britain. Lina, whose offer to drive us there we turned down, said "Just one more reason to come back." We concurred.

(2002)

A Cautionary Tale

I always wondered what the effect of an exploding airbag would be on a short person. The Saturday before Thanksgiving I found out. I had driven to Williamsport the afternoon before at the invitation of Betsy Rider who was marking the 125th anniversary of Otto's Book Store which her grandfather had founded.

It rained most of the three hour trip on Rts. 390 and 15, but as I entered Lycoming County the sun shone briefly and as always I took pleasure in my beautiful Pennsylvania hills.

With only a couple of wrong turns I arrived on Fourth Street in good time for the book fest.

It was a fun-filled three hours at one of the finest independent bookstores in the country. I chatted with the dozen other authors attending along with people who were interested in Potter County history, the logging railroad, virgin hemlock and Italian immigrants at the turn of the last century. Williamsport was once the terminus for logs floated down the Susquehanna.

Halfway through the event, large trays of food were passed around for authors and customers. Somebody pointed out the coffee urn in one corner. Despite the fact that I've given up regular brew in the evening, I was having such a good time I filled a cup once and then went back for a half refill.

Betsy invited me home to the antique-filled house where she grew up and where she and husband John reared 10 children. I was asleep by 10:30 and awake an hour later. It took some time to fall back asleep but by 5:30 a.m. I was up and dressed, leaving the house and sleeping hosts. I began looking for gas stations and coffee, eager to get home. By 6:30 I was headed north.

Day was dawning 15 minutes outside of Williamsport, and two tractor trailer trucks were crawling up the steep hill. I never pass trucks on the straight away or going down hill. But these were particularly slow, the road was dry and I went into the passing lane. I had just passed them on top the mountain when the unthinkable happened.

The SUV slid across the right lane and hit the guard rail. Smoke began to fill the interior, and fearful of fire, I reached down and found the seatbelt release. Not realizing the vehicle had flipped nor that the first truck had clipped my back corner, I crawled through the broken window on to the pavement.

Two angels of mercy with the unlikely names of Cindy Lou and Tracy, a Canadian truck driver and her friend who had been sleeping in the bunk area, came out of the second truck, and walked me back to their warm cab.

Emergency crews, a sand truck and a state trooper arrived in that order. The road was dry, I noted.

"This happens all the time once the weather begins to change," somebody said, "and right in that spot. Black ice. Notice the pine trees. They shade the road so the rain doesn't dry." Afterwards I would wonder why the DOT didn't seem to know what everbody else did and post a warning.

I had had a love hate relationship with my Pathfinder which was now totaled. An expensive gas guzzler with a car suspension it was a dream to drive, especially on abandoned railroad beds and snowy mountain roads where research had frequently taken me.

"It saved your life, " said my daughter and husband who came to get me and stopped at the body shop to claim books and clothing. I continued to give the Almighty that credit, but agreed that the SUV with its sturdy frame, airbags and seatbelts played a role. A fat lip, puffy nose and small cuts on my face and hands were the only injuries. My glasses were twisted, one lens missing. So much for the horror stories about short women and airbags.

Heretofore, because I am short and the seatbelt can hit me in the neck when I reverse, I back out of my driveway before putting it on. Sometimes I make it to the main road before I remember. No more.

If there is anything I hope to convey with this cautionary tale it is this: Never fail to buckle your seatbelt, buy the safest, sturdiest vehicle you can afford, and reserve caffeine for early morning.

(2002)

Drinking Swamp Water

Two weeks ago I joined the growing group of Americans who have had a colonoscopy. Late this spring, spurred on by the Katie Couric hype, I saw my internist who recommended the less extensive sigmoidoscopy.

I pointed out that my father and his brother had had colon cancer, and while Dad survived, my uncle did not. Did that not put me at higher risk?

No, because Dad was in his mid-seventies and my uncle in his early sixties when they contracted colon cancer, their disease was probably a matter of lifestyle, i.e. a diet heavy in meat and fat. Katie Couric's husband, the doctor further pointed out, was in his early forties and his was a familial problem.

However, two months later when it came time for my appointment, the experts had revised their recommendations. To examine only the small colon was on a par with having a mammogram on one breast.

So the first procedure was cancelled and a second appointment set up for the more comprehensive exam. I had few anxieties, being the fourth in my family of siblings to undergo it. In fact my sister pointed out it would be a piece of cake compared to the sigmoidoscopy I'd had 9 years ago with the family doctor using a rigid scope. "You're sedated for a colonoscopy," she emphasized.

"And," she added, " you no longer have to drink a gallon of swamp water prior to the test. You just drink a small cleansing cocktail followed by more water."

The truth of the matter is that I was more worried about the 24-hour fast. The comfort of food, even tiny amounts, can not be underestimated in my opinion. As it turned out, between the cocktail, the water and its effects, I was too busy to worry about eating. At the surgery center the following day, the first nurse to greet me assured me that I'd gone through the roughest part—drinking the stuff. And, she was right. From there on, it was warm blankets, booties for my cold feet, reassuring small talk and, oh yes, an IV which must have dripped minute amounts of relaxer into my veins as we waited for the gastro-intestinal specialist. I didn't even care that he was 45 minutes late.

He finally walked in and thrust a disclaimer for me to sign. I was asked to lie on my left side and woke up a half-hour or so later in the recovery cubicle with my husband next to me. The doctor came in with some colorful pictures of my innards, said everything was normal, and he'd see me in five years.

My husband went to bring the car around, and the nurse steadied me as we walked to the front entrance. I slept off and on for the rest of the day, and realized I hadn't been sedated, I'd been knocked out.

"Oh, yes, " the nurse said over the phone, "the doctor likes to keep his patients comfortable." And he had. Being one of those people who always want to be in control, had I known the extent of the "sedation," I might have balked.

Naturally I was pleased with the results and gave credit to my husband's genetically high cholesterol problem. For the past 25 years we've eaten no red meat, no fat with the exception of olive oil. And because I've been dieting for even longer, I've been fairly good about eating vegetables, whole grains and fruits. I thought of all the chicken we'd consumed over the years and the dish upon dish of pasta that has graced our table. I won't complain again.

Sometimes problems turn out to be blessings in disguise.

(c. 2000)

Your purpose in life?

Filming a TV segment that may never air, I was unexpectedly asked this past week what I thought was my purpose in life. I always thought I had my priorities straight, and the answer before a recent accident went something like this: Pass on to our family the love of God, the values, the caring and strength I received from my parents, grandparents, aunts and uncles, cousins et al.

Afterward I realized how limited my reply. Caught off guard in front of the camera, I mumbled some incoherent response, which while heartfelt, hardly expressed what I feel and know—now, more than ever.

Over the years I have come to realize the tremendous power each of us has to change another person's life whether that someone is family or a stranger we interact with for a few seconds.

A genuine smile, a solicitous word, which costs us nothing, might turn the tide for a deeply troubled person, might offer hope to those who have given up on dreams, might help a downcast person rediscover their forgotten self-worth. Conversely, an indifferent, callous, mean-spirited approach can destroy.

Some years ago when the gas and electric company turned off our power over a payment we couldn't make on time, I came to hate bill collectors. My acid tongue, ever at the ready, stood me in good stead as other creditors hounded us. Finally, when they started calling our neighbors to harass and embarrass us, I lashed out at one tormentor in scathing tones: "You poor miserable creature! Is this the best job you can find?"

Later, I would wonder about the effect of my words. Was the man who'd been hired for his ability to humiliate further those down on their luck also trying to feed his family, keep them warm? Was he, in fact, a victim also?

During this religious season,

at a time when so many are hurting, the answer I would give if asked again as to purpose: To be a conduit now and always for the love that created us, sustains us and binds us together as children of one God. Buon Natale!

(2003)

Ice Storm Revisited

The wind, rain and freezing temperatures, which glazed trees in our backyard and in various other spots around the country this past weekend, filled me with trepidation. It reminded me too much of the March ice storm of eleven years ago when we were forced from our home for eight days.

Our older daughter's in-laws took us in, along with our younger daughter, her 18-month-old baby and our old, lame dog. My husband and son decided to camp out in our family room next to the fireplace. Unfortunately it generated more smoke than heat.

A couple of nights, my husband and I slept on the floor of his office downtown. I warmed supper in a microwave oven big enough to hold a cup of coffee. In the morning we awoke with bad backs and stiff necks.

One afternoon I went home to the sun room which Old Sol had heated to a lovely 68 degrees. About four p.m. the sun moved to the west and my resting spot quickly returned to the 40 degrees found in the rest of the house.

We had hot water and my husband came home every day to shower. I couldn't stand the shock of coming out into the frigid bathroom dripping wet, and perfected the art of sponge bathing.

About six days into the ordeal, my husband was scheduled for a hospital test, which would keep him overnight. I wouldn't have traded places with him, but the thought of clean sheets and warm temperatures was tempting. The next night, after his release, we stayed with our daughter and son-in-law in an adjacent suburb where power had been restored.

In our backyard, orange-garbed electricians brought in from southern states worked steadily attempting to restore ours. And, then, late one afternoon, the lights came on, the furnace kicked in, and the television filled the family room with images from around the world.

I walked through the warm, lighted house in total amazement as supper cooked on our very own stove. Our house was a palace, a veritable wonderland. Why had I never realized what luxurious digs we enjoyed day in and day out.

This past weekend we were luckier than many people. The backyard was literally covered with small branches from the sycamores but the power lines held. And for that I gave thanks.

(2003)

The Fallen

Mid-week, I open the New York Times and find that editors have taken an entire page to show postage-sized photos of 64 young Americans who were killed in Iraq in the preceding few days. Quickly I flip the page over so I don't have to see their faces. They are so young that the term prepubescent comes to mind. But these are not little boys despite the fact that the youngest sacrificed in this travesty of a war are no more than 18, their lives finished, done, over.

They are men, albeit young men, who have been stripped of their chance to mature, to marry, raise families, become pillars of the community and live to a ripe old age. They are victims, caught in a web of lies, lies fashioned by a cabal of old men whose juices have long since dried up, men fueled by ego and the lust for power, money and God knows what else.

I try going on to the next story, but am compelled to turn back. I began searching the handsome young faces in those photographs, which have, no doubt, been doctored to cover up acne and other youthful blemishes. I pause before each image long enough to be fascinated and repelled at the same time. They bring to mind the visitors center at Gettysburg where walls covered with photos of young soldiers stare out at the unprepared and unsuspecting tourist, the faded sepia tones failing to distance the viewer from the horror of what befell them.

I try reading the rest of the paper, but can't stay focused on anything else. Eventually it is folded up and placed on the hearth where it stays for the rest of the week. In the meantime I turn on the TV over morning coffee, lunch and evening meal. The news does not get any better. More fighting, more deaths, one more book revealing the deceit and false premises upon which the nation was taken to this preemptive war. I turn the TV off, vowing to stay away from it, a promise I know I can't keep.

I grab the dog's leash and Luke Skywalker jumps to attention. We head for our favorite walking place, the cemetery across from our tract, the irony of such a retreat escaping me for the moment. It is familiar ground and has been since Clementine, long gone, was a pup.

Near the front, to the far right behind a stone wall that separates the burial ground from the street are Revolutionary War soldiers. To the left, midwalk, a cluster of WWII veterans lie beneath their markers. Here and there are stones identifying the graves of WWI soldiers. Necessary wars.

Scattered throughout are the plots of those who served in Vietnam.

The man who took us to war, I've heard, scorns intellectuals. Adams, Jefferson, Lincoln. All guilty. Doubtful, then, Mr. Bush has ever heard of Santayana's warning: Those who fail to heed history's mistakes are doomed to repeat them.

(2004)

.

The Haves versus The Have Nots

Some thoughts on the war. Are the polls about the war in Iraq accurate? Do an unbelievably high number of people in the U.S. support the invasion of Iraq? Or is the operative word here "unbelievably"?

I do not support the war, nor do most of the people I talk to, i.e., friends, relatives, neighbors. But, as I learned long ago, birds of a feather tend to flock together. So maybe my friends and I are a small minority as the newspapers and TV tell us we are. Or maybe, just maybe, the polls are being skewed.

We are totally behind the troops who come mainly from modest circumstances. And despite what some flag wavers will tell you, it is possible to do exactly that, i.e., support the troops and hate the conflict.

I am reminded of the Woody Guthrie song. *The rich start the wars and the poor die for them.* The Haves versus the Have Nots. The Powerful versus the Powerless.

The argument from the other side goes this way. The young men and women signed up for the military so they have to take what's coming to them. "They knew the score," as one woman told me, "when they enlisted."

Of course they signed up. The military, for many, has been a race leveler, a way out, a means of getting an education, of learning a trade, of getting a boot up, when family finances preclude the kind of help so many other children take for granted after high school.

Our children had that help. Our grandson's father, who served in the Gulf War, did not. Upon discharge he began schooling, financed by the G.I. bill, building on the training he received in the Navy. Obviously most of the troops being put in harm's way are those characterized as "blue collar" or "working class". All you need do is look at the families of those who have been killed, families pictured in modest surroundings, their children dying, some before they've had a chance to live.

A New York Times story notes that of those who've already lost their lives, only one was from a well-to-do family and just one had graduated from an elite college or university.

But back to this war, the cakewalk it was supposed to have been, and the polls. Earlier this year I was asked to write a history of our high school class for an upcoming anniversary with contributions coming from class members around the country. This past week a letter from a high school classmate, now living in Colorado, was in the mail. His mind was on other things besides the upcoming reunion. A life-long Republican and voracious reader of history since his teens, he reports he has been writing weekly letters to the editor of his local paper, blowing off steam.

One reason for his ire: "Mr. Bush just announced that S. Hussein was responsible for the deaths of women and children. This on the day after 100 bombing missions were flown over Baghdad. Who is the war criminal?" he asks.

I read his letter with amazement. Is this Republican an anomaly? Or are the polls being manipulated to influence and persuade? You tell me.

(2004)

On Being Vigilant

How could a smart woman (and aren't we all?) let five years lapse between mammograms? That was the question when Elizabeth Edwards, wife of vice presidential candidate, John Edwards, revealed that, yes, she'd found a lump, yes, it was cancerous and, no, she'd not been faithful about having the imaging procedure prescribed annually for women over 50.

If I had to guess, Mrs. Edwards put off the pictures for the same reason many of us do. Fear, pure and simple. My own reason for delaying was convoluted logic. I knew that heart disease kills more women than all cancers combined. Every year from the point I nailed down an appointment, usually 2-3 weeks prior to the actual date, I was anxious until the moment I was told everything was fine. Ergo, why subject my heart to such stress? I'd go every two years. But, then, somehow, the time lapse stretched to four years. Early in November I tried lining up appointments.

A month later I was able to see a new Ob-Gyn. " A thickening," she said, examining me. "Feel here." The area felt normal to me and I said so. I mentioned I had a mammogram scheduled a month away. "We'll get you one earlier," was the response and she proceeded to do so for one week hence. It was a long week. During the day I was busy with holiday preparations. I didn't have time to think about possible scenarios. But at night my imagination did what imaginations do.

Happily my appointment was 8 a.m. the day after Christmas. First the pictures, then an ultrasound "You'll be seeing Dr. Young herself," the technician said. I'd met Wende Logan-Young before, my internist sending me to her nearly 20 years ago. Since then she has become a nationally known figure in breast imaging and the number of women her clinic sees annually has grown exponentially.

Dr. Young came into the room

and the first thing out of her mouth was "Your mammogram is clear." "Thank, God," was my response and blessed her for her immediate reassurance. The ultrasound that followed confirmed the earlier results. "You're fine," she said as she left the room. Most of the women who come here are." And that is the crux of the matter.

Activist groups, those looking for research money, the American Cancer Society and the government have scared American women to death. They trumpet that one out of eight women will get breast cancer in her lifetime. Of course, by the time you read this, they could have it down to one in seven. So well have they done their job that lots of women refuse to get a mammogram including the mother of a doctor I know. That figure, one in eight, refers to the cumulative lifetime risk of breast cancer for a woman who lives past the age of 85. Thanks to the above groups, most women, especially young ones, overestimate their risk by a wide margin.

So what are we to do? (Keep in mind the same things that are good for breast cancer prevention are also good for the heart.) Remember also that the cure rate for breast cancer is now 97 percent. An annual checkup and mammogram afford the best protection for catching any problem early. You should lose weight if necessary. Obesity contributes to breast cancer. So does drinking more than one alcoholic drink a day. And you should exercise and eat right.

And, again, get that yearly mammogram. I plan to. Dumb is not a good feeling.

(2004)

A Violent Vision

I will not any time soon be viewing Mel Gibson's version of the passion of Jesus Christ.

The first reason deals with residual memories of my growing-up years. Dad required that we attend church three times a week during Lent. There was Sunday Mass with Wednesday nights given over to Lenten devotions plus a homily. Fridays were reserved for the Stations of the Cross.

Impressionable, with a vivid imagination that once kept me (and my mother) up all night with an ear ache after watching one of the "I Remember Mama" kids suffer a mastoid operation, I found the Stations of the Cross unbearable.

I would shudder through the half hour it would take for the priest to lead us through the 12 stops, attempting to tune out the stark horror of a human being put through such agony. (I would feel this way about watching any living, breathing creature subjected to torture to say nothing of a human being and the man millions call Savior.)

Gibson's film with its exploitative carnage would put me over the edge. From what I can gather from the clips promoted ad nauseam on TV, this may be the bloodiest, most violent movie ever made. The first time I saw the scourging in living color, it immediately brought to mind Mel Gibson's penchant for gore, violence and torture earlier exhibited in "Braveheart". Psychologists could have a field day here.

I submit that the extent of the celluloid scourging alone would have killed Jesus, sent him into shock or at the least rendered Him incapable of standing upright. One can't be certain. What is certain is that the film generates violence for violence's sake always keeping in mind the maxim, Sadism Sells.

The merchandising byproducts are another problem. Tee shirts and replicas of the nails that pierced His flesh and bound Jesus to the cross are but a few ways the promoters are raking in the dough.

I also have doubts about authenticity. One example: TV audiences have been subjected repeatedly to the picture of a nail being pounded into Jesus' palm. I remember being told that those crucified were nailed to the cross through the wrists, a detail that archeologists support. The fleshy palm and configuration of bones in the hand could not support the weight of the body and would have ripped away from the nail. The two bones that form an inverted V where the wrist joins the palm form a natural hook.

Then there is the alleged anti-Semitic tone. I haven't seen the film so I am no judge. From First Communion teachings at age 7, I have known who was responsible for Christ's death and it was not the Jews.

In the immortal words of Pogo, "We have met the enemy and he is us."

(c. 2004)

The Marmalade Solution?

How difficult should it be to buy a jar of orange marmalade? If the wide array of bottled fruit spread on the supermarket shelf is any indication, then the answer should be: Nothing to it. So why then should I be spending as much time as I have reading labels of the aforementioned preserves?

My initial problem came when I thought naively that the first ingredient on any such product should be oranges. Years ago I found just such a brand and there may still be some out there. But in a recent search of both imported and American brands at my local neighborhood supermarkets, the first ingredient in marmalade was one of the following: high fructose corn syrup, corn syrup, water. In one variety the high fructose variety followed by corn syrup were the first two ingredients. Orange peel and orange juice, when found, were

usually way down the list..

So why am I picking on orange marmalade? Well, I first started buying it decades ago when Keiller's Dundee came in a tall white jar with black printing perfect for pencils. (Yes, I'm one of those who often covet containers over the contents. Unfortunately now the original container has been replaced by a plain white jar and a paper label. It is wise, probably, not to dwell overlong on the current product, the company having changed hands.)

I grew to love the tart taste of marmalade made from Seville oranges on my stone-ground whole wheat breakfast toast. I gave it up when sugar started getting a bad name. But after reading in one of Jean Carper's books that marmalade was "a surprisingly good source of pectin", a substance which she reported was heart healthy, I felt I had the green light to enjoy it again without guilt.

Subsequent to reading the marmalade labels, I began paying attention to the ubiquitous message about obesity as the number one health problem in the U.S. Stories followed, blaming it on grains in general and corn in particular. A piece in the Oct. 12 New York Times Sunday magazine traces the root of the problem to our "cheap-food farm policy."

Cheap corn, writes the author, is the building block of the fast food nation. Cheap corn, he charges, is transformed into high-fructose corn syrup, pushing Coca Cola to produce the 20-ounce single serving bottle. Cheap corn, transformed into cheap beef, is what allowed McDonalds to supersize its burgers while holding down the price. The chicken nugget, he claims, is "the most ingenious transubstantiation of corn, from the cornfed chicken it contains, to the bulking and binding agents that hold it together."

But I am getting away from my original subject. This past week I ended up buying a jar of marmalade touting "50 percent less sugar" and with water as the first ingredient. There has to be a better solution.

Some time ago my husband came home with a book of 150 projects for grandmas and grandkids to do together by Peggy Epstein. Included is a microwave recipe for orange marmalade which I'm going to try. It is relatively simple requiring two ingredients: oranges and sugar.

(2004)

A Belated Conversation

My thoughts this past month turned increasingly to my father's mother, in part because of her birth date. Grandma Costa was born in 1881 in Santa Maria di Catanzaro, Italy, on Dec. 8, the feast of the Immaculate Conception, and accordingly was christened Maria Concetta. She arrived here in 1906, two years after my grandfather emigrated.

She left her parents, brothers and sisters behind, never to see them again. She also left a daughter, who died in infancy, and if Grandma followed the custom (and there is no reason to believe she did not) the child was named Carolina after my grandfather's mother.

As I continue putting together a collection of family stories, it dawned on me, more than once, that I never had an extended conversation with her–this despite the fact that she and Grandpa lived a block away in our small town, though no one would ever think of measuring it in that fashion.

I could not speak nor understand Italian apart from the few words my father taught us. Grandma could not speak English with any fluency, although she understood a great deal. Men who emigrated did far better in learning the new language by virtue of the workplace. The women, who stayed home to bear and raise children, tend the house, the garden, the animals, plus cooking and washing for boarders, considered themselves lucky if there was another woman, a compatriot nearby, with whom they could converse.

Things did not get better for my grandmother when my father, the oldest of her four sons, all born in this country, got married. The newlyweds moved in with my grandparents while the house my father grew up in was renovated for him and Mom. There was some friction. My mother was an independent 17-year-old while my Grandmother Costa understood that the wife in an

Italian marriage ruled in such a fashion her husband was the last to find out.

Later I would find out that there had been hard feelings. And it is to the credit of both my mother and grandmother that we children were none the wiser. The frequent family visits to my grandparents, along with stops I made at their house on my way home from school, were always amiable. Later, stories would trickle down, stories that saddened me. The biggest bone of contention was that my mother had named me after HER parents, when tradition dictated that Dad's mother should have had the honor. More than happy to have my doting maternal grandparents as namesakes, I never gave the supposed affront to my dad's people much thought.

Then very recently my Aunt Madeline, Mom's younger sister, in relating how her father had made her a doll bed and cupboard, mentioned that Grandma Costa had made bedding for the doll bed. In fact she still has the crocheted lace that served as the top coverlet over a spread.

Silence on my end of the phone line. My father's mother had been all kindness to my mother's little sister, who was probably nine or ten at the time. It didn't jell with the stories I'd heard.

"Oh, yes," Madeline continued. "And when Louise, (my mother's youngest sister) was born, your Grandma Costa sewed a dozen little dresses for her." Still incredulous, my heart soared. The child I was and the child still within rejoiced over the family unity. I knew my two grandmothers, living 20 miles apart, had been friends, but this said something more.

And suddenly I understood my Grandmother Costa better than at any time in my life. She had lost a baby girl in Italy, came to this country and bore four sons. Then the first grandchild, a girl, was born…Not long ago I learned that my paternal grandparents had refused to attend the christening until my father, who revered his parents, made clear that unless they did, there would be no baby visits to their home.

I put down the phone and for the first time had a real conversation with my grandmother. It was one-sided, but I've no doubt she heard.

(c. 2003)

A Night with Pavarotti

Several months ago when our daughter Johanna announced she was going to buy tickets for Pavarotti, I remained silent. She knew what a fan her father was, and thought it would be great fun for her and her husband Ron and the two of us to be on hand for this historic moment.

I, too, am an admirer, albeit a less educated one, but the thought of crowds almost always turns me off. Didn't we have perfection in the CDs we give and receive and can play for hours and hours nonstop? Then there were the television extravaganzas with the close-ups that allow us to look the maestro in the eye and watch the sweat beads form on his brow, the videos which recreate the great concerts. What further purpose would be served sitting high above the stage in a packed arena? Wisely, I kept my thoughts to myself.

The trip in to town was as I expected. We'd started very early only to encounter a traffic jam a couple of blocks away from the parking garage, not a solitary Rochester policeman on hand to help. Eventually with moments to spare, we made it into the building, and took our seats high up to be told the concert would be delayed because others had not been so fortunate. See, I muttered to myself. See.

And then the first magnificent strains of the Rochester Philharmonic Orchestra filled the huge space. And in a nano second, even before the maestro strode out on stage, I knew why 11,000-plus others had braved weather, traffic and crowds for this night.

That the Voice had diminished after forty years of performing was hardly worth commenting. Again and again the house erupted in love and admiration, no less so for the splendiferous Cynthia Lawrence of the Metropolitan Opera whose stunning "Vilja's Song" from the "Merry Widow" overshadowed even the wonderful solos and duet from "La Boheme."

Puccini, Mascagni, Verdi, Leoncavallo, were all served up. The haunting "Non ti scordar di me", a personal favorite, ended the regular program.

Would we hear the maestro's speaking voice I wondered toward the end. We would. In one of three encores he invited us, nearly 12,000 strong, to join him and Miss Lawrence in a chorus of the drinking song from La Traviata. "You all know the words," he said, "and if you don't, you can sing whatever you like." Roars of approval, standing ovations were the signatures of the night.

What was the night all about? Afterward, Johanna unwittingly summed it up best as she related how the elderly gentleman on the other side of her sang along throughout the evening, despite his daughter's admonition. He knew all the words and could not restrain himself. It was a night for Italiana, a night for music, a night to remember.

(c. 2003)

The Sopranos

Shortly after the first season of "The Sopranos," I called Time Warner and asked that HBO be added to our basic cable. I really wasn't interested in seeing another mafia story. However, my brother-in-law Ted's nephew, Michael Rispoli, a very fine actor, was in it and curiosity got the better of me.

We began to watch the summer reruns and were fascinated by the production, finding it compelling entertainment, this in spite of our reservations about a film in which once again Italian-Americans are portrayed as gangsters.

Ironically, the reason for our watching it in the first place was short-lived. Michael, who had the role of Jackie, the don, died of cancer in an early episode. Nevertheless we kept watching. We waited for the second season to begin, uncomfortable with the material, but sucked in by the creative, slick, professional approach. When we questioned this portrayal of Italian-Americans, one more stab to

the heart, we soothed ourselves by noting it was written by an Italian-American, Chase deriving from Cesare.

The episodes were screened at 9 p.m. Sunday nights. We have a young grandson living with us, and I kept worrying about watching a channel in which sex and violence are not merely tolerated, but celebrated. But I told myself he was in bed by the time the show came on.

I watched perhaps half of the new episodes, uneasiness growing as the violence increased. Every new doubt was met by a newspaper story or TV critic lavishing praise on the series. The Emmy award shows, which originally ignored "The Sopranos" as possibly too much of a threat to network TV, changed their tune. I looked forward to an episode set in Italy. Anticipating beautiful settings, if nothing else, I got sick to my stomach as filth and corruption ruled. This along with an episode in which the "protagonist" was shown coupling with a "bada-bing" strumpet in a frontal view of her that opened my eyes literally and figuratively. My God, what was I doing allowing this kind of garbage in my house?

What if the grandson got up and began flipping channels? An even more important point: what was I doing watching something that perverts every value I hold dear including my heritage. We cancelled HBO. The show continues to win more raves and more awards. Apologists for the treatment of Italian-Americans keep coming out of the woodwork. I know what I saw. Excrement is excrement. Gilding it does not change its essence.

Old Christmas Cards

I was cleaning out the basement storeroom looking for the tree holder when I came across a bag of old Christmas cards…A pack rat I am, but why this bundle? I soon found out. Among those from neighbors who had long ago moved away was a card from my mother's mother. There was a note: "Just heard your Mom is somewhat better. I was so excited I forgot to finish my prayers. Love to all, Your Gram."

The card was postmarked Dec. 22, 1981 My mother died two days later on Christmas Eve as had her maternal grandmother in 1935.

There is no good time to lose your mother—not a glorious, sunny spring day, not a dreary, rainy Fall day and most certainly, not Christmas Eve—a day of joyful anticipation. That night we took our three children to Midnight Mass, and as the priest began to recite the list of souls for whom to pray, my husband grasped my hand firmly to counter the reality.

Sometimes I dream that my mother is still with us, fragile but on the mend from the cancer that no doctor detected during the two years prior to her death. Morning, when it comes, I lose her all over again.

Clutching Gram's card, I leaned against the doorjamb and indulged a little, tears mingling with a prayer to Mom to throw her arms around her mother, now in heaven with her, and comfort her for all the losses of her life.

In September I published the book about our family I have been writing for years. To use a term much in vogue it was an epiphany. From her sisters, brother and her first cousins I learned much about Mom's early life and the anxieties that beset her after losing an infant brother and sister to diphtheria and pneumonia.

Afterward, more stories surfaced, tilting the skewed picture of her teen years I had formed. Mom's younger sister, Madeline, told me how Mom, then 13, came home from DuBois that first year away at high school, and belted ala Sophie Tucker, "I'm going to love you like nobody's loved you come rain or come shine."

I relished the image of her prancing about their small house in the woods, imitating the last of the red hot mamas. As a kid I remembered her singing "Some of these Days, you're going to miss me, honey," Tucker's trademark song.

Earlier this month I went to Smethport to sign copies of "Growing Up Italian in God's Country," and met several of Mom's friends who had known her as a young housewife and mother. A phone call from a man in Ohio, who had known her family, interrupted the signing. He had another story about Mom's teen years. "Your grandfather caught my brother Tony trying to kiss your mother. He was ready to go for his shotgun."

I love hearing these stories about my mother before she was my mother. Much better memories than those of her illness. Toward the end of the signing session, an old friend walked in and when she saw me did a doubletake. "For a minute, I thought it was your mother," she said and added, "She was beautiful." I nodded. And will forever be in her family's memory.

(c. 2001)

Passings

Dad's 90th birthday party was coming up in July and the family was planning a celebration as usual. Only this time it would involve more people. Because Dad had been in business in Smethport, since 1950, building both a supermarket and a super hardware, and because he still went to the office every day, we would have an open house for the town of 2,000 people.

A deposit was sent to the fire hall where such functions take place in the small Pennsylvania town. Last year the new pastor, Father Ted Marconi who had joined us at the family camp for the picnic supper, had offered to celebrate Mass there this year. My sisters were planning the menu, grandchildren, and great-grands, 9 of them, would put on a little program to honor Grandpa as they had last year.

Then a couple of weeks ago Dad's angina, which he'd dealt with since his bypass surgery 19 years ago, flared up. We blamed it on a change of medication. There were several trips by ambulance 18 miles over the mountains to the Bradford Hospital emergency room. And two weeks ago, there was another. No not a heart attack, just angina, we were told. And Dad began to get better, inquiring about his greenhouse, making small talk about the day to day events in his life. But there was another episode and tests showed substantial heart damage. Earlier he'd been asked if he wanted to be resuscitated should it become necessary .

"I want to live," Dad said.

It was the same spirit, the same interest in life that had kept him productive for so long. Despite bypass surgery, a bout with colon cancer and removal of a kidney, he looked, acted, thought and spoke like a man 20 years younger. Handing the day to day business of the stores over to my brothers a few years ago, he still occupied himself in his life's work.

He'd gone to work at age 12 after school in Austin, Pa selling half barrels of flour from a railroad car to Italian families. An Irish grocer wanted a boy who could speak to Italian immigrants in their own language. The grocer, Bill Gilroy, became Dad's mentor and good friend.

"When my laborer father offered to send me to college," Dad recounted, "I was too smug and said, no, a decision I've regretted all my life." Instead he worked for Gilroy's Grocery for 26 years before setting out on his own. He ended up with some of the largest stores Potter and McKean counties had seen to that point, selling his children's bonds when banks refused him credit, borrowing from his father and my mother's mother to build and rebuild after a fire demolished his first store in Roulette. He battled prejudice the way he did every other challenge, by working harder. And always he was proud of his Italian heritage, grateful to his parents for the sacrifices they made in coming to this land.

His work was his passion, surpassed only by his family and his faith. But he knew how to have a good time. He loved the wilderness of his Potter County birthplace and Smethport home, loved the hills and mountain streams. Trout and bass fishing, growing flowers, vegetables and trees, woodworking, cutting brush around the camp's 40 acres were leisure activities.

Later he discovered large print books and began reading novels for the first time. (Heretofore any spare time was devoted to reading supermarket manuals and fishing magazines.) Biographies were his favorite, however, and he enjoyed the memoirs of James Michener, Louis Lamour, Luciano Pavarotti, Russell Baker, Pope John Paul II, among others.

Dad took his last breath in the early morning hours of Palm Sunday, 1997 with all five of his children gathered round, joining my mother who had left us on Christmas Eve 15 years before.

His friends were many and devoted, friends who came to tell us what he had meant to them. Among them: my former sister-in-law who told us, "A great man has died."

"The best," added my stepmother. Conclusions with which none of us would argue.

(1997)

Other Essays

Don't Kiss Me Goodbye! I'm Going With You.

An earlier version of this article ran in St. Anthony Messenger July 1994. The editors eschewed my title substituting "Holy Vacations"!!! Had they traveled with our trio they would know our vacations were something other than sacred, although blessings continually showered down upon us.

My husband Carmen and I were getting ready to run some errands one weekend. We planned to leave Johanna, 4, and her brother John, 2, at home with Carmen's mother, Helen, who was visiting from Albany. I dropped a kiss on our napping toddler and move purposefully toward our daughter. Standing her ground, she waved me off. "Don't kiss me goodbye," Johanna protested. "I'm going with you."

And go she did, despite our original intention,—not just then but at every feasible opportunity. So did John and their younger sister, Cara, when she came along. We took our children with us wherever we went, in part, because we couldn't find anyone up to the task of riding herd on them and be secure in the knowledge both the kids and caretaker were safe. Their combined antics terrorized more than one sitter. Both our families lived three to four hours away so there was no help there. And raging anxiety on my part made it necessary to keep them in full sight for peace of mind. Still we harbored no regrets.

Carmen was an editor and I, a reporter, then columnist, on metropolitan newspapers. We loved the excitement of the city room, but were more than ready to settle down and take on the task of raising a family.

When Johanna was born I gave up my job critiquing TV for

the Democrat and Chronicle to be a full-time mother, the days of working from home via computer a long way off. Carmen proved to be a caring and hands-on father, taking on any and every baby chore from changing diapers to walking the floor at night. We delighted in her and could talk for hours on a single subject: our baby.

When Johanna was two and no other children on the horizon, we began adoption proceedings, a fairly easy matter then. A year later, five-month-old John came home to us. His arrival was delayed by an ear infection. That first night he cried on and off. Not knowing whether it was the different surroundings, the new arms holding him close or the lingering infection that caused the wails, we held and rocked him through the wee hours. By morning, any strangeness had worn off. Adoption was merely a term: He was ours and we were his. Johanna was as thrilled with her baby brother as we were. She quickly established a nightly baby race despite the fact that John at five months could only roll sideways and shriek, "Ah-bah" as they frolicked on the living room carpet. They were so alike in coloring and features strangers would stop and say, "You can tell these two are brother and sister." And they were despite the absence of any biological link.

A few years later, Carmen became the first lay editor of the Rochester diocesan newspaper and ran a series of pictures of black and biracial babies who were up for adoption. "What do you think?" my husband asked. "We want another baby," he said, "and these babies need a home." After much thought, prayer and uncertainty, I confided in my sister, Thomasina, who in effect told me to do what was in my heart. "Yes," I said to Carmen and once more the adoption procedure began.

Then in a far shorter time than it had taken the first time, our caseworker, one Ethel Keefe, whom we shall ever think of as our chain-smoking fairy godmother, called to say, "I've a baby here with the cutest mug you've every seen."

On a slushy March day we four trooped to the Catholic Family Center, in downtown Rochester, John in Carmen's arms, Johanna's hand in mine. Outside the Center, a street cleaner deep in snow removal outside the building, peered at us as we entered. A short while later we emerged, this time with a third child, a three-month old baby girl in a pink bunting. The street cleaner, leaning on his shovel, raised his eyebrows. "Boy, you people must like kids."

We named our new daughter Cara, "dear one" or "beloved" in Italian. And she was. Cara's first trip with the family was an Easter visit to my parents' home in Smethport in northwest Pennsylvania. Earlier when we'd told my father about our daughter's bi-racial background, he said, "She's just a baby isn't she? A baby who needs a home."

"Why she's beautiful!" my mother exclaimed as she undid the pink bunting and gazed down at the serene *caffe latte-colored* features. Mom stuck a tiny matching bow in Cara's soft brown curls, then took our infant down to the family supermarket to show her off to employes and customers. It did not escape our attention that our daughter was the only person of color in the entire town of 2000. Later on Cara's first trip to Albany to visit Carmen's mother and family, our baby was greeted with the same unreserved warmth and love.

From the time our children were infants, we took them to church with us until they started disturbing those around us. We tried leaving them in the church nursery up to the day we went to pick up John, a rampaging toddler. The women managing the nursery couldn't find him. John, 2-1/2, had escaped and was wandering in the crowded parking lot. We found him surrounded by cars, some of them beginning to pull out. That was the end of leaving our children in such facilities. The good-hearted church women were no match for our inventive kids.

Our young brood were also particularly creative in terrorizing sitters. John once brought in the garden hose to water the living room carpet (in his defense the 70's green shag did simulate grass). Another time the phone rang waking us at 6 a.m. It was our neighbors, Bud and Donna Seaberg, who informed us that John, who had unlocked and opened the kitchen door, was naked and playing on the swing set in the backyard. For her part, Johanna, eager to demolish her good girl image, engaged in an applesauce war with Chris Peterson, the boy next door. Not too naughty except the applesauce was still in the jar. One young sitter was reduced to tears the time Cara, a toddler, escaped out the front door to frolic (also sans clothes) around the yard. It wasn't long before we wore out the good will of most of the neighborhood teens who baby-sat for us. Diane Seaberg, 13, who lived next door remained faithful, confiding that as a precaution she removed her contact lenses before coming over.

Although we publicly moaned about our children's misdeeds to family and friends, secretly we thought them to be the brightest, funniest and most beautiful children God had ever given to any couple. We knew ourselves to be blessed beyond belief. In our eyes our kids were better sports than star athletes, more trustworthy than civic figures and more entertaining than TV and movie celebrities.

Our lives revolved around them, all creative firstborns, full of limitless energy. Blessed with good health, they presented us with only one problem: how to keep one step ahead of them.

Because of our limited funds, family vacations consisted of, well, visiting family or going camping at state parks around the country. But sometimes, we were able to combine vacations with Carmen's editorial assignments.

One such outing included a reception for newspaper editors and their families at the Iranian embassy in Washington, D.C. before the cleric-led government took over. The ambassador, a relative of the shah, was delighted as Johanna reported she'd written a school report on Iran. She was rewarded with a kiss. With our attention focused elsewhere, Cara, 5, took the opportunity to raid the resplendent, linen-covered tea table of all its chocolate-coated strawberries.

One year, Carmen went to Italy to cover Fr. Joseph Beatini's 25th anniversary as a priest, in his hometown of Licciana. When Carmen returned, he proposed taking all of us to Italy the following year. It was a land of great beauty, history and culture, he persuaded. But most importantly, it was the land of our religious and cultural heritage. (Actually when we included the kids' English, Irish, Iranian, African and Dutch backgrounds, we formed our own United Nations!)

"We can't afford it," I hedged, having acquired a fear of flying about the same time I achieved motherhood. "And the house needs all kinds of repairs, to say nothing about the car."

"The dollar is strong, and the food in Italy is as cheap as it is delicious," came the retort. "We can see the Roman forum, the coliseum and have an audience with the pope." All arguments ceased. What was a new roof compared with the glories of Rome?

I sat white-knuckled through most of the night flight and when the pilot announced at daybreak that the Alps could be seen to the right, causing passengers to rush to the windows, I was sure the lopsided weight would cause us to fall out of the sky. The kids found Mom's terror hilarious.

Our three took to Italy like sauce to linguini. In Milan, our first stop, Cara charmed the dour-faced desk clerk at our tiny hotel by waving and calling "Ciao" as we wedged ourselves into the wardrobe-sized elevator. The woman's severe countenance dissolved into a smile that threatened to crack its sculptured contours.

"Bye, bebe," the woman cooed. Any concerns about how Italians might view our biracial family were put to rest.

Then in Rome, our youngest traveler scandalized the staff of a two-level, elegant bookstore by sliding on her bottom down an imposing marble stairway. When the manager stroked one index finger with the other— the universal sign for "shame on you"— the unremorseful culprit threw up her hands and gurgled, "No *capisce*." It was not Cara's only Italian word. She also mastered *burro* summoning the waiter when her brother and sister wanted butter with their *panini* and, of course, *gelato*, preferring *fragole*, strawberry ice cream.

One highlight of the trip was our "audience" with Pope Paul VI in a room with about a thousand other people. The kids seemed to understand the significance of the occasion and took it in stride as they did the rest of the trip.

It was an other-worldly trip in many ways. On a quiet afternoon with no guards in the Roman Forum to deter him, her father lifted Cara up to stand on one of the pedestals, formerly occupied by statues of the vestal virgins. In Piazza Navona, where we visited the famed Tres Scalini more than once for Tartuffo, the kids were delighted one evening to find an Afghan hound standing on its hind legs at the bar enjoying their favorite. The owner stood idly by as the dog licked up the concoction of ice cream, chocolate shavings, hazelnuts and cherry topped with whipped cream.

In Venice, nine-year-old John mastered the city in an hour or so, disappearing periodically into the tiny streets to find the best pizza. Johanna, a grown up 12, rivaled her father in stamina by sightseeing from sunup to sundown in Florence, soaking up the Uffizi's Botticellis and gelato cioccolato with equal enthusiasm. Every lunch and dinner consisted of pasta in some form, often in the small trattorias frequented by natives.

A particular delight was a side trip to Pompeii. The kids trooped through the ancient, unearthed streets, stopping to take note of the baths, examining the inner brick structure under the worn stucco of an Ionic column, remarking on the ruts worn in the stone streets by the chariots, marveling over the remains of the baths and the House of the Vetti brothers.

So successful was the trip that the kids kept clamoring to be taken again to Italy. And a couple of years later we were able to take our second once-in-a-lifetime trip, accompanying Carmen on a working trip to Rome. The dollar was even stronger and our knowledge of how to travel on next to nothing had increased. At the time, I was editor of a biweekly, and my earnings had gone into a pot for just such a possibility.

This time our Roman holiday took place during Holy Week. We stayed at the Raphael, at the time a shabby genteel hotel with marble floors and oriental carpets, just steps from Piazza Navona, and where down the hall from us on the second floor was actor John Houseman. Cara boldly knocked on his door and he, granite-faced charmer that he was, scribbled his name on the piece of paper she proffered. During a visit to the Vatican museums, she was similarly enchanted at finding Charlotte Rae of TV's "Different Strokes" in line just ahead of us.

Early on Sunday morning, we walked from The Raphael over the Ponte Sant' Angelo bridge, the winged statues guiding us on our way to Easter Mass in St. Peter's Piazza. The roar when Pope John Paul II ascended the balcony after Mass to welcome 300,000 people in 42 languages sent thrills through all. The brilliant sunshine, the crush of the crowd under the watchful eyes of the apostles atop the basilica had us pinching ourselves in disbelief. Hearing the pope deliver in person his traditional blessing urbi et orbi (to the city of Rome and the world) crowned the experience.

Then without warning, or so it seemed, our family trips were over. The older kids were in high school and could not simply be lifted out for a couple of weeks of culture and good times. We also became aware that they no longer found us as interesting, funny or companionable as we found them.

But it didn't take long for them to begin traveling again, this time on their own. Johanna headed for Yale, seven hours away. John, a student at nearby Nazareth College, went to France for a year of study. Cara married straight out of high school and moved with her sailor husband to the navy base on Whidbey Island off the coast of Seattle 3000 miles away.

The first break was the hardest, each succeeding one only somewhat easier. Every time one of them left, I, hands clasped together, wanted to cry out as Johanna had so many years before: "Don't kiss me good-bye. I'm going with you."

But parents are bound by different rules than four-year-olds, so I held my tongue and most of my tears. Hadn't this, after all, been our goal all along: to raise, loving, strong and responsible adults who could stand on their own?

With their impatience barely concealed, they would kiss their father and me, chiding us as they detected a trace of moistness, then eagerly leave to discover worlds beyond what we had shown them.

They wrote us letters, called us on the phone and made visits that seemed too short, but it wasn't the same. The fabric of our lives seemed frayed and in tatters.

But as time passed, we discovered that the threads we had woven over the years were not so easily unraveled. We had taken our children with us, instilling our beliefs, values and sense of family in them. Now they were taking us with them in spirit, if not in body.

Our family gatherings are times to reminisce and rejoice in the gift of each other, to relive our trips as we sit around the dinner table. "Remember how we walked forever to see the *Last Supper* in Milan then all the way back to the Duomo?" Johanna says. "John was hungry on the way back so Dad stopped in a trattoria and we walked down the Via Magenta eating sausages and panini?" We smile and nod as she continues, "Remember when we thought we had lost our bags on the train to Venice and Cara thought we had to jump off when it slowed in Verona to go find them? And how John found them in the luggage car?"

Then somebody always says, "Wouldn't it be great if we could all go again together?"

"Yes," we chorus, and then grow silent. We know that, even if we could, it wouldn't be the same.

Then another favorite anecdote surfaces and we are off again, reliving the bits and pieces of our family history, bound by love and memories, if not proximity.

In a quiet moment I look around the dining room and see them as the children they were and as the responsible, loving adults they are now. Any regrets dissipate in the gift of the here and now. Had they not grown up, we wouldn't have our beloved grandchildren.

Another in a million prayers of thanksgiving wings its way upward.

The End

A Visit From Beyond

(Previously unpublished)

Our son-in-law, Ron Bartlett, who comes from Iowa farming stock, put in his garden this year and when the deer got through eating the delicacies, he ended up with a large crop of green tomatoes. I asked for, and received, a peck plus, our own garden having been overrun by my husband's tarragon and sweet basil.

Years ago I made green tomato relish every fall. It is tangy, sweet and wonderful on hamburgers. Best of all, the finished product bears no resemblance to its green tomato origin, a definite plus to my way of thinking.

I stopped making the relish when we stopped eating hamburgers some years ago. But now with turkey burgers and low fat hot dogs on the menu I had the urge to make another batch. Leafing through the cluttered and long-ignored folder of handwritten favorites, I came across the relish recipe.

It literally took my breath away. For it was written in my mother's strong, graceful handwriting and seeing it was akin to a visit from beyond.

For years after Mom died, I would dream she was calling me and the sound of her voice saying, "Patricia," every familiar nuance in place, would wake me from sleep and leave me wondering if it, indeed, had been a dream.

Coming across her handwriting on an old birthday card to one of our children, on a squirreled-away note from her, or a recipe, makes as strong an impression as the dream, her essence embodied in the strong, uniform letters that would do a penmanship teacher proud.

Gazing at her handwriting, I could see and feel the smooth roundness of her trim, white arms, smell the bath powder fragrance of her, hear the wry note in her voice as she made some blunt

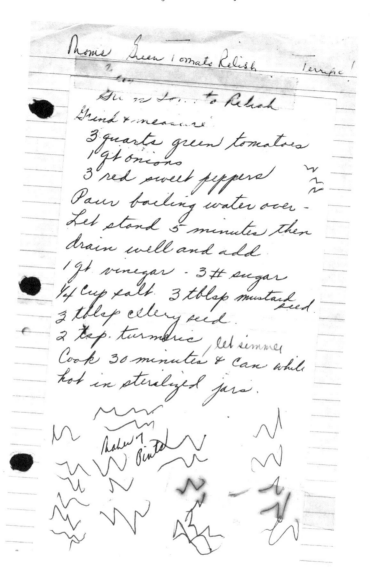

observation, the dry wit changing to loving softness if she were cuddling a baby or indulging one of her grandchildren.

When we went home to Smethport in the northwestern Pennsylvania hills, or Mom and Dad came to visit in Rochester, Mom and I were ecstatic the first hour or so, delighting in each other's company, catching up on news of brothers, sisters, grandparents. But within a short time, we'd be exchanging barbs, so much alike were we. For years after she died, I regretted the memory of our verbal tilting until I realized that's all it was: jousting that defined and upheld our different perspectives, but took nothing away from the respect and love we felt for one another.

As I searched through the pockets of the loose leaf binder, I came across other recipes in her handwriting, wonderful treats she'd cooked for us when we'd all been at home and then written down and sent across the miles at my request.

There was nutmeg feather cake, melt-in-your-mouth Hawaiian lemon pie, a unique salmon loaf, Swedish tea log, sweet dill pickles. A bonus to the handwriting, they are accurate reminders of her creativity and prowess as a cook and of the way Mom best expressed her love.

As I picked up the relish recipe to refresh my memory as to what other ingredients were needed, I spotted a series of little red waves made with a ballpoint pen encircling Mom's directions. Drawn by one of my children before she or he could write, the waves did not obscure the recipe but merely enhanced the margins like embellishments on a 10th century manuscript.

I remembered the annoyance when I first discovered the art work and how I'd scolded the small culprit soundly although exactly which child it was escapes me. Now the red waves are almost as precious as Mom's handwriting—our children gone from our home to hearths and kitchens of their own.

On a cold, dreary September morning, I pushed quartered green tomatoes through a hand grinder, added cider vinegar, sugar and spices and set it to cook. Soon the bubbling mixture filled the house with the irresistible, tangy smell. A sample spoonful was sweetly tart and delicious on the tongue and the batch and a half netted enough pints to last through many a burger or hotdog feast.

When I finished, I carefully gathered up the recipes and stored them in the loose leaf cookbook. Along with Mom's recipes are some other family classics from Aunts Madeline and Louise and my grandmothers, Maria Concetta Corcoglioniti Costa and Anna Policastro Borelli, written by them or dictated to other family members.

Realizing anew what I held in my hand I turned away from the cook book shelf, and placed the folder next to treasured family albums. No longer just a recipe collection, it is family history, a record to be cherished and preserved. (*See the recipe section at the end of the book for ingredients and directions.*)

Upon A Winter's Night
A Christmas Story

Green ropes of pine twined with jeweled lights, arching above the village Main Street. Alex trudged along in the early dusk, head down, hands stuffed in the pockets of his hooded jacket. He fingered the bills and coins with little hope. Most of the stores were already closed for Christmas Eve.

Across the street the five and dime was suddenly thrown into darkness, and he heard Mr. Higgins call out to a departing customer, "Merry Christmas!"

Illustration by Ron Bartlett

Alex angrily kicked a mound of light snow, the resulting squall frosting his face and clothing. It would be anything but merry at his house. "And it's all my fault," he muttered.

The picture of 9-year-old Sarah's tear-streaked face refused to go away. If only he hadn't been such a know-it-all. It hadn't mattered years ago when his Sunday school teacher told the class that dogs and cats didn't have souls. But that was before Cubbie grew old.

The dog had died two weeks ago. "What a time to go, Cub," he'd heard his dad say. The mostly black Lab had been a present for Alex on his 7th birthday and was already full-grown when they'd rescued her from the shelter.

"As black as a bear," Alex said, and dubbed her Cubbie. For a while they were inseparable, Cubbie sleeping on his bed, following Alex on his paper route. But as the years passed, Cubbie slowed down, unable to keep up with Alex and his pals.

Alex pretended he didn't care when Cubbie took to sleeping in Sarah's room or thumped her heavy Lab tail on the oak floor when Sarah came home after school. She would get up despite the arthritis in her hind legs to limp to his sister and be smothered in kisses.

For the last year, at Sarah's pleading, Dad had carried Cubbie upstairs at night. It tore at Alex to see his old friend in such shape, but he pushed what he knew was coming to the back of his mind.

Alex didn't allow himself to cry the night he and Dad took a sick Cubbie to the vet's or the next day when they brought her home in a black plastic bag. He didn't cry when he and Dad dug the hole down near the border rocks where wild violets bloomed in spring. Not even when they threw in the last shovels of dirt, and he saw his father's face was wet.

Of all of them, Sarah took it the hardest. She cried through meals and sobbed herself to sleep at night. Then, just when she seemed to be doing better, Alex came home one afternoon to discover she'd been in his room, rummaging in his desk.

When he realized Sarah had taken the picture of a 7-year-old Alex and Cubbie both wearing party hats on that special birthday, he'd become a wild man. He confronted her in the front hall.

"You've no business in my room!" Alex shouted. "How dare you take something without asking."

It's a surprise. A surprise for..."

Sarah's attempt to explain enraged him more. "I'm sick of you wailing and carrying on about that old dog, spoiling Christmas for Mom and Dad, for all of us. Forget about Cubbie!"

Sarah's brown eyes were stormy, her thin frame ready to do battle. "I won't ever forget her! Not till I die and go to heaven and be with her."

"Don't be stupid," Alex said, wanting to hurt her, to punish her for not letting Cubbie go, and making it impossible for him to stop thinking about her. "Dogs don't go to heaven. They don't have souls."

Sarah stared at him, the fight gone, her bottom lip quivering. She was silent, then her voice barely audible. "Where do they go?"

"Nowhere," he said feeling like a monster, already sorry for what he had done. "They become nothing."

Sarah turned ashen, raced up to her room, almost knocking Mom over as she came down the stairs.

"Alex, how could you?" his mother asked. "I expected better of you."

Later he heard her tell his dad, heard Dad mumble something about Alex's loss. He went to his room then, burying his head in his pillow.

Alex tried to make amends, taking most of the money he was saving for new hockey equipment. He bought the miniature blue and white tea set Sarah had been eyeing in the antique shop window. It was wrapped and under his bed along with the gloves for his mother and a book of Robert Frost poems for his father.

Somehow Alex knew that even the much-coveted tea set was not going to make Sarah smile Christmas morning.

His parents assured Sarah that no one knew for sure about animals and heaven, but she kept looking at Alex as if his was the only word that counted. He refused to meet her gaze, his anger now a lump of guilt lodged in his throat.

His mom kept Sarah busy icing cookies, his dad requesting her exclusive help to decorate the tree on this, the day before Christmas.

They made a production of it, Mom bringing in mugs of hot chocolate and gingerbread men, carols filling the room. Eventually the tears stopped, but Sarah's face didn't lose the pinched look. Then she opened the last box of ornaments, found the black needlepoint dog against the red stitchery, and started all over again. Alex saw the helpless look his parents exchanged and went up to his room.

Taking his remaining savings, he started for the village, stealing out the front door so no one could call him back. Just maybe he could find something else that would make up for what he had done.

With relief, he saw the drug store was still open. Through the glass door he eyed Mr. Castelli busy in the back with a lone customer. A leather strap of sleigh bells jingled as Alex went in. He prowled the aisles, picking up and rejecting a small, silver-backed hairbrush, a music box with a ballerina atop, a leather case of colored pencils. He shook his head. Nothing was right.

He had given up hope of finding the one special thing that would put the light back in Sarah's eyes when he spotted the clearance table. Almost hidden in a cluster of dusty angels was a miniature black dog, perfect but for a chipped tail.

Alex picked it up, his spirits rising as he marveled at the resemblance to Cubbie. The china dog had the same kind of red collar Sarah had bought for Cubbie, and a round, gold ID tag. But it was the comic tilt of one ear and silly half-grin that did the trick. Cubbie was the only dog that Alex had ever seen smile.

"How much?" he asked Mr. Castelli, who'd taken off his white coat to count up at the front register.

The druggist, who had known Cubbie, took the miniature and turned it over, then handed it back. He closed the cash register with a bang. "Pup needs a good home. Merry Christmas, Alex."

Alex hurried the six blocks in the darkness, turned a corner and saw their Christmas tree glowing in the bay window, the colored lights beckoning him home. His mother called from the kitchen when he opened the front door. "You're late for supper, Alex. Where have you been?"

"I'll be right down," he said, and tore up the stairs. In his bedroom, he found a piece of green tissue paper. Later, after Sarah went to sleep he would put the dog in her stocking.

At the table his parents stared at him, his mother exclaiming over his red cheeks. "We were worried about you. Running out like that."

"I had something to do," Alex said, letting the mystery hang in the air. No one commented. He knew they were still upset with him.

That night, when Sarah went to bed and his parents were wrapping gifts in the den, he tiptoed down the stairs.

The strains of *Gesu Bambino*, his mother's favorite carol, resounded softly through the house. Flowers blossoming upon a winter's night... Yes, it was a night for miracles, he thought, and realized the lump in his throat was gone.

In the dim light of the shining tree, the pine fragrance permeating the room, Alex headed for the bookshelf where Sarah's stocking was anchored. He stopped, a new thought taking hold.

Yes, he thought. *Yes.* And taking the green tissue off the china dog, he moved across the room to a small table.

Christmas morning went as expected. Sarah tore paper off box after box, giving him a small sad smile when she got to the tea set. His dad exclaimed over the book of poems, urging Alex to open some gifts from his own pile.

He picked up one, keeping his gaze on Sarah, then ripped off the paper to find a scrapbook filled with pictures of Cubbie. New misery filled him as he remembered his outburst and the grief he'd caused his sister.

They were almost finished when he saw Sarah glance across the room, blink in disbelief, then jump to her feet. Bounding to the end table, she let out a shriek. Alex followed his puzzled parents to Sarah's side.

There in the manger, closest to the crib, crowding out the lambs and the cow and the donkey, was the little black dog smiling down at the baby Jesus.

Carefully, Sarah reached in and brought out the miniature. Alex could hear the rush of air as she sucked in breath. "Mom, Dad, look! It's Cubbie. Even the red collar and gold tag. Look at her ear, oh her funny, floppy ear."

Sarah turned from one to the other. "Who did it? Who found Cubbie?" His mother and father shook their heads, Alex giving nothing away.

Sarah's excitement grew as she put the china dog back next to the crib, her eyes wide and luminous.

"But that means...if none of you put it there," she cried, "that means ...it's a miracle. *A miracle!*"

For the first time in a week, his mother smiled at Alex. "Not that kind of miracle, Sarah," she murmured.

"I think your brother had something to do with this, Sarah," his dad said, putting an arm around Alex's shoulders.

Sarah searched Alex's face as he stroked the tiny animal with one finger. "I found the dog at the drugstore last night just as Mr. Castelli was closing. It did seem sort of a miracle, looking so much like Cubbie.

"Then afterward I kept thinking about finding her—you know, at that particular time, when you needed...when I needed..." He took a deep breath.

"Anyway, that's when I figured out that if God took the trouble to fill an animal...a dog like Cubbie...so full of love that it just spilled over on everybody, He never intended for Cubbie to become nothing."

Sarah's face was a sight, eager but cautious. "You think then...that Cubbie, the real Cubbie is with...?" She broke off looking upward, then back at Alex as if he alone had such an important answer.

Last night's carol played again in his head. Flowers miraculously blooming 'mid the winter's snow. A much-loved pet they'd see again someday. He had wanted to believe and now, unexpectedly, he did.

He looked at Sarah. "How could Cubbie not be there?" he said slowly, feeling his smile grow, matching the china dog's. "How could she not?"

The End

(First published in the "Democrat & Chronicle" 12/25/96)

Recipes

The following recipes were written about or alluded to over the years in both my newspaper columns and my book, "*Growing Up Italian in God's Country: Stories From the Wilds of Pennsylvania*." I always felt they, and many more than are given here, deserved a book of their own. But in the interim, here are those which evoke the most cherished memories, grouped according to the family cook most associated with the dish. The food a family cooks and eats traces its history as much as any facts and figures. It also documents the lifestyles that the land, their economic status and work dictated. Manual labor called for substantial meals. And our parents, grandparents and great-grandparents were intimately acquainted with hard work.

Here are some of the dishes that sustained them.

Vittoria Casa Policastro

(Maternal Great-grandmother)

I have to admit that I don't know if this is the bread recipe that my maternal great-grandmother used. She joined my great-grandfather Giuseppe in Pennsylvania in 1895 from San Gregorio Magno, Province of Salerno, Campania Region, Italy. Vittoria arrived with my grandmother Annie Borelli's four older siblings, Maria, Laura, Gregorio and Veet and began baking bread in her field oven to sell to the crewmen on the Buffalo and Susquehanna logging railroad, the tiny depot a stone's throw from their farmhouse. She used 100 pounds of flour a week, selling the loaves for 5 cents a pound. However, because Grandma and Mom both used this recipe, it only follows that it was handed down from Vittoria. This bread not only sustained my grandmother's childhood family, but my mother's and mine. It was eaten at every meal, but sometimes Grandma Borelli made pizza, or foccacia, a flat bread made from the dough with black pepper and perhaps a thin slice or two of onion on top. As a surprise on a cold winter's day, Mom would pinch off a piece of the rising dough, roll it out and make fried bread when we walked home from school at lunchtime in Austin. While these intrepid bakers used cake yeast, the recipe is adapted for dry yeast granules. My mother and grandmothers never made small batches of bread, but directions here are for two loaves.

WHITE BREAD
Ingredients
2 packages dry yeast
1 cup lukewarm water
1 1/3 cups warm water
1 cup scalded milk
3 tablespoons sugar
1 tablespoon salt
2 tablespoons shortening or oil
9 to 10 cups flour

Directions
Dissolve yeast in 1 cup lukewarm water. Stir in warm water, scalded milk, sugar, salt, shortening and half of the flour. Beat until smooth. Mix in enough remaining flour to make dough easy to handle Turn onto lightly floured board and knead until smooth and elastic. Place in greased bowl; turn greased side up. Cover and let rise in warm place until double, about 1 hour.

Punch dough down and divide in half. Shape each piece into loaf, sealing ends under loaf. Place seam side down in greased loaf, pan. Let rise until doubled. Heat oven to 400 degrees. Place loaves on low rack. Bake 30 minutes or until tops are lightly browned and sound hollow when tapped. Remove from pans, brush with melted margarine and cool on wire rack.

FOCACCIA
Use recipe above. After first rising, make one loaf bread, l foccacia oval. For foccaccia roll out 1/2 recipe of dough until 1/4 inch thick. Let rise 30 minutes or so. Brush with olive oil and top with 1/2 thinly sliced onion and black pepper. Bake 20 minutes or until golden brown.

FRIED DOUGH
Pinch off enough rising dough to make 8 inch round. Roll into circle. Fry both sides until golden brown in small amount of vegetable oil. Butter and add maple syrup or sprinkle with sugar and cinnamon.

Maria Concetta Corcoglioniti Costa

(Paternal Grandmother)

BAKED MACARONI

This dish was brought to America from Santa Maria di Catanzaro, Calabria, by my paternal grandmother, Maria Concetta Corcoglioniti Costa. It was served every holiday, both in my grandparents' home and in our house, as it was my father's favorite. My sisters Thomasina and Judy have mastered it. With this dish my grandmother would serve green salad, homemade bread and roast chicken with a delectable stuffing consisting of bread, cooked ground beef and hard boiled egg.

Ingredients and Directions

Cook 2 pounds of rigatoni until al dente. Drain but do not rinse. Place in large oven proof dish (Mom used an oval aluminum roaster which I will ever associate with this recipe.)

In a separate container beat eight eggs and 3/4 cup of Parmesan or Pecorino Romano cheese together. Add 6 to 8 cups of cooled tomato sauce and blend well. Add to rigatoni. Bake in 350 oven for hour or until the custard of sauce, cheese and eggs is firm and macaroni is slightly crusted.

N.B. Cousin Nancy Viscomi serves extra sauce to top individual servings.

* * *

PIGNOLATE

Grandma Costa did not make many desserts, but we were assured of pignolate at Christmas time. The platter of these tiny deep fried nuggets of egg-rich dough, coated in honey and decorated with sprinkles would be arranged on a table covered with Grandma's crocheted lace tablecloth in the double living room. Next to it would reside a decanter of Grandpa Tom's homemade red wine. Much later I would learn that these nuggets are also called struffoli. Next door neighbor Yvonne Yockel also lent me a newspaper article giving the recipe for pignolate in which the instructions were to shape the nuggets as pine cones. I was not sure of the exact translation of pignolate. I knew the root word was from pinolo or pine nut and assumed it was because some cooks sprinkled pine nuts instead of candy bits on the honeyed nuggets. Whatever they're called they're delicious, one of my son's favorites, and always bring to mind Christmas celebrations at the white house at the head of Turner Street in Austin, home of our Costa grandparents.

Ingredients
2 cups flour
3 eggs
1 tablespoon sugar plus 1/2 cup sugar
1/2 teaspoon baking powder
1 cup honey

Directions
Sift flour, 1 tablespoon sugar and baking powder together. Beat eggs until foamy and add to flour. Work to soft dough. Cut into four pieces which you roll into four ropes. Cut off into one inch pieces. Dust lightly with flour, shake off excess. Heat peanut oil or other vegetable oil in large frying pan and fry a few nuggets at a time until golden brown. Transfer with a slotted spoon to paper toweling to drain. Cook honey and 1/2 cup sugar over low heat until sugar has dissolved. Add the nuggets a few at a time. Turn to coat with honey on all sides. Transfer nuggets to platter and mold into desired shape. Add sprinkles. Let harden

*   *   *

CRISPEDDI
I have never made these filled savory treats, also known in Southern Italy as crispelli but my mother, grandmothers, sisters all have. My sister Judy says they are akin to zeppole sold in the New York City area. My dad loved them and my brothers Sam and Paul have been accused by certain members of the family of hiding some for later enjoyment. Unfortunately the Brothers Costa sometimes

forgot they'd squirreled them away and petrified crispeddi would be discovered months later in their all too-secret hiding places.

What follows are Thomasina's instructions to Paul who wanted to make them himself. Thomasina uses the food processor to knead the dough. It can be tricky to get the dough just right, so unless you are handy with the food processor, use the instructions for kneading the dough by hand. Grandma Costa and Mom filled some with tuna and some with anchovies. Note that some can be fried without filling and sprinkled with confectioner's sugar to eat as a pick-me-up dessert.

Ingredients
6 cups flour
1 1/2 cups very hot water
2 packets of dry yeast
1/2 cup warm water
2 tablespoons sugar
1 teaspoon salt
1/2 cup Crisco

Directions
Dissolve Crisco in boiling water. Add sugar and salt and stir. Cool mixture further by adding 1/2 cup water. Add yeast and stir until lumps dissolved. Blend with flour and mix well. Turn onto lightly floured surface and knead until smooth and elastic. (N.B. Thomasina notes that if you have a granite or marble surface, roll out the dough with no flour to ensure seams don't come apart during the frying.)

Put in lightly greased bowl, place in warm spot and let rise until double in size, about 60-90 minutes. Punch down, flip over and let rise again, about 30 minutes.

Meanwhile prepare tuna and/ or anchovies. This recipe makes 25 to 30 crispeddi. "I (Thomasina speaking here) use four cans of white albacore tuna squeezed really dry, chopped up until flaky and placed in bowl with several layers of paper towel under fish.

"I use 2 cans of fillet of anchovies also using paper towel to get all of the oil off them. The oil causes the seams to open up while they are frying.

"When the dough is ready, pinch off a piece the size of an egg and roll in shape of rectangle on floured surface. Lay a single anchovy on it and pinch ends and sides together. Make sure your hands are not oily! To make tuna-filled crespeddi use about 1 tablespoon of tuna and proceed as below.

"Lay seam side down on unfloured cookie sheet. Leave space between so they will rise properly. Fill one sheet, cover with towel and put in warm spot to rise for 30 minutes and continue making others.

"Put three inches of oil in heavy cooking container (I use my pressure cooker as it is heavy) and heat for 10-15 minutes until hot but not smoking. Test by throwing in a small piece of dough. If it browns immediately it is too hot.

"When you slip them in the oil try to place them seam side down. I used a big fork and slotted spoon to keep them from turning over. When golden brown remove with slotted spoon and drain on several layers of towel in a flat tray."

*　　*　　*

Thomasina

EASTER BREAD

As delicious as her other Calabrian dishes were, Grandma Costa hit her stride, in my opinion, with her braided, dense, anise-scented Easter Bread. Each of her sons' families received as many loaves as there were children in the family. We were given three and I can still remember our delight when Dad would carry in the fragrant loaves on Holy Saturday, stopping at our grandparents on his way home from work at Gilroy's Grocery to pick them up. They were works of art, resembling baby buntings, shiny braided crusts drizzled with pastel frosting, an egg at the top. On Easter Sunday a large braided round, studded with eggs, would rest on a side table for those unable to wait for Grandma's holiday meal. I loved Easter Bread (and still do) fresh, stale, toasted, untoasted for breakfast, lunch, dinner and snacks. And to my joy, so do our children and our little grandsons. I never made it until after I was married and kept misplacing the recipe. I sent home for it more than once and I treasure the note and prickly aside my little sister Judy, then 12, sent me in response. She wrote:

Judy

GRAMMA'S EASTER BREAD
(See if you can hold on to it for more than a week this time—J.C.)

Ingredients
6 eggs
1/2 cup margarine
2 tablespoons sugar per egg (2/3 cup)
1/2 cup milk
2 packets of yeast dissolved in 1/4 cup warm water
2 teaspoons salt
1 teaspoon lemon extract
Anise seeds or oil (optional)
Add enough flour to make a soft dough. (5-6 cups)
Bake 40 minutes at 325 degrees. Makes three loaves.

Directions
Scald milk and add margarine and sugar. Blend well. Let mixture cool then beat in eggs, one at a time. In separate bowl, sift flour and salt together. Add lemon and anise flavoring to egg mixture. Add flour to egg mixture one cup at a time until dough is no longer sticky. Add more flour if necessary. Too much flour will result in a dry loaf. Knead by hand until dough is elastic and smooth. Cover and set in a warm place to rise for about 2 hours. Divide into 6 or 9 equal balls depending on whether you want to make 2 large or 3 smaller loaves. Roll each ball into a long rope about 15 inches. Braid three ropes together. Brush with beaten egg. At top of each loaf place raw white egg pointed end down to simulate face. Let rise until double in size. Bake in 325 degree oven for 40 minutes or until loaves are golden brown. Cool on racks. When cool, drizzle with colored confectioner's sugar to resemble pastel ribbons. Finished loaf will resemble baby bunting. I sometimes use colored pencils to give the egg facial features. Note: In speaking with Dad's first cousin, Nancy Corcoglioniti Viscomi, 92, just before publication, Nancy said she also made Easter bread shaped like a fish. Giving the fish an open mouth, she inserts an uncooked egg in the opening before baking. Nancy grew up in Great-Grandmother Annunziata's Calabrian home in Santa Maria di Catanzaro.

* * *

STUFFING FOR ROAST CHICKEN

This recipe came from Aunt Frances Costa who wrote that "This was the way I was told to do it. I never measure so I can't tell you how much of anything. Just experiment". Thomasina did experiment, "winging it," if you'll excuse the expression, for a 12- pound turkey and the resulting stuffing was a winner with her family . The measurements are hers.

Ingredients
8 cups stale bread crumbs.
4 hard-boiled eggs
4 tablespoons tomato paste
4 tablespoons water or more depending on how moist you want the stuffing
1/2 cup grated Pecorino Romano cheese
8 ounces of ground beef
2-3 cloves of garlic

Directions

Place bread crumbs in large bowl. Add finely chopped hard boiled eggs. Brown ground beef and finely diced garlic in 1 tablespoon oil (use extra oil if the beef is very lean) and add to bread and eggs. Add grated cheese. Dilute tomato paste with water and add to mixture. Blend well, cool and stuff chicken or turkey.

Maria Concetta Corcoglioniti Costa

Anna Policastro Borelli

(Maternal Grandmother)

My Mother's mother Grandma Anna Policastro Borelli grew up at Hammersley Junction, a terminus for the Buffalo and Susquehanna Logging Railway, just north of Wharton, Pa. The first child born to Vittoria and Giuseppe Policastro in this country, Donata, as she was baptized, was one of 13 children. The family was too poor to buy macaroni and subsisted on their mother's homemade bread and the potatoes their father grew by the acre, fried in lard. When Anna married Grandpa Patsy Borelli who came from the Roman countryside at the age of 19, they settled in Conrad and macaroni and beans, *pasta fagioli*, a seminal Roman dish, became their nightly fare. Grandma made homemade noodles on special occasions, the family's favorite.

HOMEMADE NOODLES

This recipe came from my niece Mary Buonocore Kaldany, a museum textile conservator, but who follows in her mother Thomasina's tradition as an all around good cook. Mary preserved this recipe from her "great-gram".

Sister Judy tells this story about noodle-making. When Gram was in her early eighties, Jude begged Grandma for lessons in how to make the noodles. They were to be a present for Dad's birthday on that hot July day. "All right, honey," Gram said, "but you'll have to do the rolling yourself—my old ticker isn't so good anymore." Beginning with a piece of dough about 5" in diameter and 3" thick, Jude rolled and rolled and rolled. After about 20 minutes, and with perspiration beginning to roll down Judy's face, the sheet of dough had spread across half the table.

"Are we almost done yet, Gram?" she asked.

"No, honey, you've got a ways to go. Want me to take over?"

The fear of giving her grandmother a heart attack prevented Jude

Don't Kiss Me Goodbye! I'm Going with You

from handing over the rolling pin, and she spent another 10 minutes of fairly ineffectual labor. When asked again if she wanted her grandmother to take over, Judy surrendered the rolling pin, which was actually a broomstick that Grandpa Patsy had sawed off and sanded over 60 years earlier. Gram, bent over with arthritis, took the rolling pin, and became a whirling dervish

In less than 5 minutes the sheet of dough completely covered the table and draped over the side. With a few more deft motions, the huge sheet of dough had been folded, cut into strips, and hung over the broomstick to dry for that night's supper.

Ingredients
4 cups of flour
2 eggs
1 teaspoon salt
1/4 cup (or more) water.

Directions
Mound flour and salt on large floured surface. Make a well and break in eggs one at a time, beat lightly with fork and blend with water. Keep pulling in flour until all is used. If too sticky add a bit more flour. Blend well and knead until dough is smooth and elastic. Cover and let rest for 5-10 minutes. Using a rolling pin, roll out pasta in a circular sheet until paper thin and three feet across. Sprinkle lightly with flour . Roll up and cut strips about 1/3 inch thick. Unfold and place to dry. Cook in boiling salted water until al dente. Fresh pasta cooks in a minute or two so test frequently for desired texture. Serve with tomato sauce.

* * *

SPAGHETTI SAUCE
Technically this is a sauce made of tomatoes, and should be referred to as tomato sauce but years of calling it spaghetti sauce has been ingrained in my mind. Everyone in the family has a different method for making it. My mother and grandmothers canned their own tomatoes, so that there were scores of jars upon their shelves to use throughout the winter months. They would thicken the tomatoes with tomato paste and sometimes tomato puree. I did this also for a number of years until I realized we like the sauce made from commercially canned tomatoes at least as well, and it's a lot less

page 186

work. I do not use paste or puree, but a good quality crushed tomato, infrequently an Italian import including the famed San Marzano tomato. The most flavorful sauce in my mind is made by browning a couple of skinless chicken thighs, then adding a large can of quality crushed tomatoes, a minced clove or two of garlic, a tablespoon or two of extra virgin olive oil and fresh basil leaves. After our first few trips to Italy, and enjoying the fresh flavor of sauce there, we cook ours as little as possible, between 30-45 minutes. No more all day simmering!

* * *

MARINARA SAUCE
Ingredients and Directions

This meatless sauce again depends on good quality tomatoes. Saute several cloves of garlic and 1/4 cup of finely minced onion in 1/4 cup extra virgin olive oil until translucent. Do not brown. Remove garlic. Add crushed tomatoes and fresh basil leaves. Simmer for 20 minutes. Use to top pizza shells, for pasta, for vegetables such as fresh stringbeans, eggplant Parmigiana. The uses are seemingly endless and the sauce also freezes well.

* * *

PASTA FAGIOLI
Ingredients and Directions

Score and brown small piece of salt pork in heavy container. Rinse, sort and cover with water 1 pound navy beans with medium onion, peeled carrot and salt pork. Bring to boil and turn off heat. Let stand one hour. Then cook on low to medium heat until tender. In separate container cook until al dente a pound of small macaroni, e.g., ditalini, elbows, tiny shells. Combine beans and pasta in desired proportions with some of the onion and carrot if desired. For white pasta fagioli use 1 or 2 cups of the bean liquor, depending on how soupy you want the dish. (If using canned white beans, I add canned chicken broth.) For red pasta fagioli use a blend of bean liquor and a small amount of marinara sauce. Top with grated cheese, e.g., Pecorino Romano or Parmesan. My husband loves to add dried oregano to the dish, giving the flavors time to marry before serving. (My Roman-born grandfather wanted this every night, and according to my aunt Louise, Gram added a bit of bacon grease and tomato paste to the bean liquor.)

* * *

CHICKEN AND BISCUITS

Chicken and biscuits with gravy and mashed potatoes alternated with the homemade noodles and sauce at Grandma Borelli's Sunday dinner table. We children, my same-age aunt Louise and I, little sister Thomasina, little brother Sam and I vied for the drumsticks and the gizzard and liver!

Directions

Cut up whole stewing chicken, cover with water and cook in heavy container. When chicken is done, lift out and make gravy. Heat stock to boiling. If necessary add water or canned broth to supplement liquid. Place four tablespoons flour and eight tablespoons water in small covered plastic container and shake to lump-free consistency. Pour into stock, salt to taste and whisk until gravy cooks and thickens, about 10 minutes.

* * *

While chicken is cooking make
BAKING POWDER BISCUITS
Ingredients and Directions

Sift together 2 cups flour and 2-1/2 teaspoons baking powder and 1 teaspoon salt. Cut in 1/4 cup shortening and stir in 3/4 cup milk Blend and turn out on floured surface. Knead lightly and cut into circles with floured cutter. Bake on ungreased sheet for 10 minutes or until golden brown.

At table, ladle gravy and chicken over split biscuit for individual servings. Serve with mashed potatoes, new peas, green salad. For dessert Lemon Sponge Pie.

* * *

LEMON SPONGE PIE
(In Gram's handwriting to Thom)

Ingredients
Line pie pan with crust.
Filling
1/4 cup butter (I use oleo—Gram)
3/4 cup granulated sugar.
3 1/2 tablespoons flour
2 egg yolks
Grated rind and juice of one small lemon.

Directions

Mix as you would a cake, then add 2 cups milk. Stir well and fold in stiffly beaten egg whites. Bake 45 minutes at 350 degrees. "Thom, if your oven is accurate and pie browns too fast, reduce temperature to 300."

Good luck and love from

Your Gram

* * *

Grandpa Patsy Borelli, foreman on the B&S and later the B&O, took a square silver lunch pail with lift out tray to work. When we children were visiting, he made sure he'd leave something for us to find at the end of the day. We'd run to meet him as he came down the path from the tracks which wound around and up the mountain. There in the tray might be a piece of the lemon sponge pie or one of Gram's date cupcakes, unfrosted yellow cake or custard in an orange oval dish. The recipe for the muffins, incidentally, was acquired, Gram said, when she was in the hospital for gallbladder surgery.

Anna Policastro Borelli

GRAM'S DATE MUFFINS

These are so moist and delicious I can mentally conjure them up as I copy the recipe sent to me by Gram in 1967.

Ingredients
1 cup dates cut fine.
Pour 1 cup hot water over dates and let stand.
1 scant cup sugar
1 tablespoon shortening
1 egg
3 tablespoons cream
1 teaspoon vanilla

Directions
Beat egg, sugar, shortening and cream together. Add date mixture.

Sift together and add: 1 1/2 cup flour, 1 teaspoon baking soda, pinch of salt. Blend well and bake 20 or 25 minutes until brown in 350 oven. (*Nut lover that I am, I add 1 cup chopped walnuts.*)

* * *

BUTTERMILK PANCAKES

As children visiting our grandparents in their Conrad home alongside the maple-lined Sinnemahoning Creek at the foot of the mountain, we expected buttermilk pancakes for breakfast. We were not disappointed. The aroma rose from the floor vent in our young aunts' bedroom directly over the kitchen's wood cook stove. Slumbering softly under patchwork quilts and sloped ceiling, we would wake to the tantalizing smell and tumble out of bed and make our way downstairs. Gram in her starched dress and fresh apron would look at our sleepy faces and flyaway hair and tease, "The more they come, the worse they look." Any sting in her words was erased by the plates she put in front of us. Spread with butter from Betsy the cow, and maple syrup Gram made from tapping the trees and cooking down the sap, the buttermilk pancakes were thin, chewy and delicious.

Ingredients and Directions
Beat well 1 egg
Add 1 1/4 cups buttermilk

Add in and beat 1/2 teaspoon baking soda
1-1/4 cups flour
1 teaspoon sugar
2 tablespoon soft shortening
1 teaspoon baking powder
1/2 teaspoon salt

Beat until smooth and pour on hot griddle, turning as soon as they begin to puff up.

*   *   *

SATURDAY NIGHT FRIED CAKES

When Dad closed Gilroy's Grocery in Austin Saturday nights at 9 o'clock we would head for Conrad and Mom's family via Costello, Wharton and up the East Fork Road. It was a deliciously scary ride as the electric lines stopped abruptly at Costello. We drove in darkness most of the way with only light from an occasional kerosene lamp shining from the windows of the scattered houses. Sometimes we'd see a green glow, eyes of wild animals caught in the car's headlights, behind the fence of the Susquehanna State Forest. Our grandparents' home was a beacon in the night, kerosene lamps illuminating the downstairs. The twin doors to the living room and dining room were thrown open at the sound of the car. Loving arms greeted us, and soon we were inside, the delicious aroma of freshly brewed coffee and fried cakes permeating the house. When I wrote to Gram one winter many years later for the recipe, she did not respond immediately. But then after Christmas she forwarded this card signed "love and best wishes" from former Conrad neighbors Sarah and Roy Purdy on which Sarah had written: *Dear Anna: Was so glad to hear from you. Hope we can get together soon. Am sending you the recipe. Have a blessed Christmas.*

Ingredients
2 eggs beaten
1 cup sugar
1/3 cup melted shortening (I use oleo)
1 teaspoon vanilla
nutmeg
1 cup milk
4 cups flour
4 teaspoons baking powder

Directions

"I (Sarah) mix them up and put them in the refrigerator overnight or chill good. They are easier to roll without using so much flour. I roll and cut them all and let them sit while I heat the oil to fry."

My young aunt Louise's job was to shake some of the doughnuts in granulated sugar, some in confectioner's sugar in a brown paper bag. We children were allowed a heavily sugared, diluted drink of coffee and canned milk, wonderful for dunking purposes.

At some point Gram sent both Thom and me this recipe for Fried Cakes made with buttermilk. At the bottom of Thom's she wrote *P.S. I would use butter the size of an egg in case you don't have cream.*

Ingredients and Directions

1 egg
1 1/4 cup sugar
4 tablespoons cream
1 cup buttermilk
1/2 teaspoon soda
1/2 teaspoon baking powder
1 teaspoon salt
4 cups flour or enough so you can handle the dough
Roll out and cut. Fry in deep fat.

*   *   *

HOMEMADE ICE CREAM

Ice cream was a big treat. Our refrigerator in Austin would hold a pint from Hernquist's drug store—if you took out the ice cube trays. There was no electricity at our Borelli grandparents' home in Conrad, and perishables were cooled in the spring house or set in the snow during winter. But ice cream could be had! One wintry weekend day, Grandpa and our dad drove with several of us kids to the B&O Horton Run water tower. Water dripping down from the tower had formed a frozen pond. With an axe Dad and Grandpa broke the ice into chunks and placed it in a burlap bag. We drove back down the East Fork Road to home and in the back yard Grandpa crushed the ice with the flat side of the axe. The wooden ice cream maker stood ready on the back porch. Inside Gram had readied a cooked mixture of milk, cream, sugar, cornstarch, eggs and vanilla flavoring which went into the clean silver cylinder. It was placed in the wooden ice container, the dasher inserted and capped and rock salt and ice packed around it. Grandpa, Dad and my young uncle Alfred alternated turning the handle. It seemed to take forever, but eventually the top was taken off, revealing soft ice cream. A few more turns and again the dasher was lifted out and handed to Gram who saw that our ready spoons were filled. Later, we ate larger portions out of pink Depression glass berry bowls. Was it the best ice cream ever? We thought so. The following makes a custard-like treat.

Ingredients
1-1/3 cups sugar
1 teaspoon cornstarch
Dash of salt
3 cups whole milk
2 egg yolks
1 pint heavy cream
1 teaspoon vanilla extract

Directions
Beat egg yolks lightly and set aside. Combine sugar, cornstarch, salt and whole milk. Cook over medium heat for one minute. Let cool and pour 1 cup of mixture into eggs. Stir and combine all of egg and milk mixture. Cook over low heat until slightly thickened. Stir in whipping cream and vanilla. Pour into silver cylinder and proceed according to ice cream maker directions.

Patsy Borelli's lunch pail which he took to work first on the Buffalo and Susquehanna R.R and later, the Baltimore and Ohio R.R.

Margaret Borelli Costa

(Our Mother)

Does anyone not think their mother is the best cook in the whole world? We've known some individuals who've hinted quite the opposite. But my sisters and brothers have no doubt *our mother* was without parallel. Madeline, Mom's younger sister and our dear aunt, who lived with us while attending high school in Austin, says that everything Mom did, cooking, cleaning, ironing, tailoring, had to be perfect. And I can testify that whatever I attempted as a kid whether it be wiping off the table after supper, making my bed or mixing up a batch of cookies, Mom would come behind me and take corrective action. I had no problem with her redoing everything. I figured my talents lay elsewhere, e.g. reading under the covers with a flashlight throughout the night. Mom showed her love with cooking, not words, and no family member was left out. When my then husband-to-be started coming home with me, Carmen was wowed by Mom's made-from-scratch dinner rolls. From then on he could be assured of a panful of huge, fluffy rolls at every visit. Sticky buns, a delectable dessert version of the rolls, and my favorite, greeted me when I came home each time from Villa Maria in Erie during my freshman year.

It was difficult paring down the number of favorite dishes that Mom made for us for inclusion here. She cooked Italian, American, German, the last picked up from friends with that heritage. I leaned heavily here toward the Italian dishes she'd learned from her mother and mother-in-law, and which Dad loved so much.

GNOCCHI
The directions are straight from Mom as recounted in a letter to Thomasina. We loved them as kids and remember having them at "Grandma" Cercone's home on the hill above us as well as at home. We called them "rats" or what sounded like "suditches". Much later I

would discover that the Italian word for mice is "sorice" pronounced "so re-chey". In short, the finished gnocchi looked like toy mice to us children and one of our grandmothers had dubbed them thusly in Italian turning the tiny mice into benign rodents!

Ingredients and Directions

Boil two large baking potatoes, peel and let them cool. Rice (or mash) potatoes, mound them, make a well and add 1 beaten egg and enough flour to make a dough that isn't sticky. Then work it like noodle dough until it's smooth. Cut into strips, roll into ropes and cut off little pieces (about an inch long) and using your thumb or finger dig a large indent in each. If they are sticky when you dig them, flour your board and dip your fingers in flour and let them dry a while before you cook them. Boil in salted water until they come to the surface, a matter of a few minutes. They should be tender but not sticky. Top with marinara sauce and grated pecorino Romano cheese.

*   *   *

BAKED CHICKEN AND VEGETABLES

This was one of Mom's standards which we all loved. A nice change from pasta and rice. Figure on at least two extra pieces of chicken and two more of each vegetable than the number of people you will be serving.

Ingredients and Directions

Layer chicken parts (I like skinless thighs and drumsticks best for this recipe) in shallow roasting pan. Peel and cut potatoes into wedges. Peel and quarter medium-sized onions. Peel and cut carrots into thick strips about four inches long. Add to chicken. Drizzle with extra virgin olive oil. and bake at 400 degrees for about an hour or until both vegetables and chicken are tender and starting to brown. Baste chicken and vegetables throughout with drippings. I can't decide which is my favorite vegetable in this dish--probably the onions which become carmelized.

*   *   *

CANNED SWEET PEPPERS AND SAUCE

This is a wonderful treat teamed with homemade crusty bread for a quick lunch, meatless supper or snack. I've never canned them per Mom's handwritten instructions, but have combined fried peppers and marinara sauce for sandwiches or to top pasta, one of my husband's favorites.

Ingredients and Directions

Pick or buy your peppers and let them sit a week or so before using. (It helps to dry up some of the moisture) Have an equal amount of tomatoes and make sure they are dead ripe. Blanch them (dip in boiling water for about two minutes then put them in cold water). Peel and core them making sure you get all of the green or white spots of the core out. Squash each one with your hand and they will cook better. Put some basil in your tomatoes and also some salt. Cook slowly, and don't scorch them, until they begin to thicken.

Clean your peppers and slice lengthwise. Put at least one quart of vegetable oil in a deep pan so oil is 2 or 3 inches deep. Fry a few at a time. As soon as they start to turn brown, lift them out and put in a colander to drain. Salt each layer. You should do a batch of hot peppers to mix in for flavor. Mix peppers and tomatoes together thoroughly. Place in jars, using a funnel. Be very careful not to get any oil on the mouth of the jar and make sure all air bubbles are out of the jar. Run a table knife down the side wherever you see a bubble and the air will come to the top.

Follow instructions with jar lids and put in water bath and boil for 20 minutes to seal them.

*   *   *

MOM'S MEATBALLS

Whenever I eat some small, hard, marble-like meatballs made from ground beef, I think of Mom's *polpette*, my father's favorite. Her delectable meatballs were large, tender and often contained a mixture of lean ground pork, veal and beef. What really set them off was the large amount of stale Italian bread she used, which made for a soft meatball. The bread, half a loaf or more, would be soaked in water for perhaps 10 minutes, then squeezed dry and blended into the ground meat along with eggs and grated cheese. So well did she combine the ingredients, that never a hint of bread could be seen in the finished product. They were shaped into large balls 2 1/2 inches across and fried in a cast iron frying pan in a small amount of olive oil, then transferred to a huge pot of simmering sauce to finish cooking, adding fantastic flavor to the sauce. For a large family gathering, Mom would use as much as 3 pounds of meat or more, but I've cut this down to use 1/2 pound each of the beef, pork and veal.

Ingredients and Directions

Place 1/2 pound each of lean beef, pork and veal in large mixing bowl. Soak 4 thick slices of stale Italian bread in water for 10 minutes. Squeeze dry and add to meat. Add two beaten eggs and 1/4 cup of grated pecorino Romano cheese, 2 cloves finely minced garlic, 1 teaspoon salt. Blend well so no trace of bread, egg or cheese is visible. Shape into balls and fry in two tablespoons olive oil, turning until browned on all sides and insides are no longer pink. Remove with slotted spoon and drain on paper towels and add to sauce.

The polpette accompanied whatever pasta Mom cooked, but they also make fabulous meatball sandwiches using either a crusty hard roll or two slices of Italian bread. Heap with meatball and sauce and sprinkle more grated cheese on top.

*   *   *

SPAGHETTI WITH TUNA
Ingredients and Directions

Spaghetti with tuna was a staple(as was Salmon Tomato Loaf) on meatless Fridays. Sister Thomasina insists it requires a thinner sauce and I have come to agree with her. If you are using home canned tomatoes, do not add puree or paste to thicken. Ditto for using commercially canned plum tomatoes. This recipe calls for tuna packed in olive oil, found in Italian import stores. If you have none available, drain the tuna (both water-packed and that packed in vegetable oil) and discard juices. Add 4 tablespoons of extra virgin olive oil. If the tuna is packed in olive oil, drain into frying pan and add 2 tablespoons more. Saute two cloves of garlic until translucent, then discard. Add tuna and 1 large can of plum tomatoes to heated oil, breaking up both slightly with fork. Simmer for 20 minutes. If you happen to be growing Italian parsley in your garden, add 1 tablespoon finely minced herb to the sauce just before topping spaghetti. I can't remember Mom cooking any pasta except spaghetti with tuna, but this sauce would be equally good on penne or any other macaroni.

*   *   *

SALMON TOMATO LOAF
Ingredients
2 cups red salmon
1 1/2 cups crushed canned tomatoes

1 tablespoon melted butter or vegetable oil
1 teaspoon sugar
salt and pepper
I onion finely diced
1 3/4 cups bread crumbs
1 egg well beaten

Directions

Flake salmon. Remove bones. Combine all ingredients. Empty into oiled baking pan. Form into loaf. Bake at 350 degrees for 45 minutes.

*   *   *

SPANISH RICE

A few months ago, one of my brothers sent out a request for Mom's Spanish Rice. I used to make it for my kids and remembered diced green pepper being one of the ingredients. You should have heard the e-mail groans. Here, courtesy of Judy, is the "authentic" recipe along with her recollections about how she and Paul approached it. "I have a feeling we watched Sam do it first and then imitated him. When Mom doled out a big spoonful onto our plates, it was straight out of the pot and steaming hot.   It became almost ritualistic—you never took a bite from the big mound on your plate, but flattened it into the thinnest possible layer, covering the entire surface of the plate so it would cool more quickly. Then we started at one end of the circle, pushing our forks carefully through the diameter of the circle of rice, creating a road. Then we cut another "road", dividing the circle into four quadrants. Later on we got more creative and made more interesting designs…"

Ingredients

1 tablespoon vegetable oil
1 medium onion, chopped
1 lb. of ground chuck beef
1 cup of rice
1 can of Campbell's tomato soup
1 large can of whole plum tomatoes
(Mom used her own canned tomatoes, but I think the large can is equivalent)

Directions

1. Saute onion in vegetable oil.
2. Add ground beef and brown.
3. Crush the whole tomatoes (you have to use the whole because otherwise there won't be enough juice to cook the rice); blend in tomato soup and add to ground beef mixture.
4. Add the rice and with heat on medium high, bring to gentle simmer. Cover; lower heat to maintain the simmer. Cook for 45 minutes, stirring occasionally so that the rice doesn't stick. Check occasionally to see if a little water is needed to prevent sticking.
5. Serve with crusty bread and a green salad.

*   *   *

GREEN TOMATO RELISH

The very name of this relish turned me off—until I first tasted it many, many years ago. My husband Carmen and daughter, Cara, are also very fond of it. We use it on hamburgers and hotdogs, sandwiches and whatever else needs a little zing.

Mom got this recipe from our next door neighbor in Smethport. Elsie and Doc Murray (Dr. William) lived next to us on Main Street. I've referred to the relish in more than one column over the years, but never credited Elsie. So thank you, Elsie. Or just having returned from another trip to Italy, I am moved to say, *grazie mille,* a thousand thank yous.

Ingredients and directions

Grind and measure:
3 quarts firm green tomatoes.
1 quart onions
3 red sweet peppers
Pour boiling water over vegetables. Let stand 5 minutes then drain well.
Add 1 qt. cider vinegar
3 lbs. sugar
1/4 cup salt
3 tablespoons mustard seed
2 tablespoons celery seed
2 teaspoons turmeric
Bring to boil and reduce heat. Let simmer 30 minutes and can while hot in sterilized jars. Makes 7 pints.

*   *   *

PICNICS, WE LOVE PICNICS

As much as I loved Mom's every day and holiday cooking, I lived for the picnics we had. When my brother Paul and sister Judy were toddlers, Mom and Thomasina would pack the car on summer afternoons and with the babies, head up the dirt road, past Jeanne and Bernie Vossler's farm to Prospect. There they would set up a kitchen on top of the mountain overlooking Smethport. Home from college, I was helping Dad at the store and he, brother Sam and I would close the family's Main Street store, at 5:30, and head up the mountain. We'd arrive to find supper under way. Fried cubed potatoes were crusting satisfactorily in a cast iron frying pan and hamburgers just starting to sizzle on the grill. Best of all the blackened coffee pot was perking away. I know of nothing that tastes better than coffee brewed and savored outdoors, the aroma, flavor and body enhanced by the mountain air. One evening it began to rain and we pulled the folding table under a huge spreading maple tree and continued our al fresco repast.

In earlier days, in Austin, we picnicked every time Dad went fishing. We'd head up toward Odin, down to Costello, or over to Keating Summit. The meals were impromptu affairs, a blanket thrown down next to the stream, though not so close it would disturb the trout—or the fisherman. Mom would pack sandwich meat, bread, Dad's homemade root beer and the remains of whatever dessert we'd had the night before. There were also picnics at Cherry Springs, Patterson Park and at Sizerville where we kids would swim in the ice- cold spring water that fed the large pool.

But the most delicious picnic food was the kind Mom prepared for a really festive occasion, e.g, a get-together with parishioners of our small mission church, St. Mary's, in Roulette. We would head to Cuba Lake, some of the kids in the back of Ed Lacher's plumbing van. And once our family went to the scenic Grand Canyon park in Wellsboro where Dad found an arrowhead next to the park table. Mom pulled out all the stops for this kind of venture. There would be a roaster full of baked chicken, her scrumptious potato salad, beans baked from scratch, fluffy yeast rolls , carrot and celery sticks and for dessert a picture perfect apple or blackberry pie accompanied, of course, by freshly brewed coffee on the outdoor fire.

MOM'S POTATO SALAD
Ingredients and directions
Boil 8 potatoes, cool and peel. Hard boil and cool four eggs. Cut potatoes into medium-sized chunks into large bowl. Peel, cut eggs and add to potatoes. Cut several stalks of crisp celery into bite size pieces. Dice 1/2 sweet onion. Gently blend potatoes, eggs, celery and onion. Top ingredients with one tablespoon sugar. Pour 1 tablespoon cider vinegar into sugar. Add 1/2 to 1 cup of Miracle Whip salad dressing and 1 tablespoon prepared yellowed mustard. Blend all ingredients. Refrigerate for several hours before serving.

My brother Sam, Aunts Madeline and Louise each make their version of the above potato salad with slight variations.

Sam proffered this version

Louise Gerardy Potato Salad 1983
Boil potatoes with skins on.
Peel while still warm for ease.
Hard boiled eggs.
Pickles: sweet, diced.
Green stuffed olives, cut.
Sweet onions, diced.
Miracle Whip salad dressing to match quantity.
Dab of prepared salad mustard to taste.
Small amount of sugar to taste.

Louise

* * *

BAKED CHICKEN
Wash and pat dry chicken parts. Brush with oil. Place in roaster and cover tightly. Bake at 400 degrees until tender about 45 minutes to an hour. Brush with oil several times during baking. Remove cover last 20 minutes to brown.

* * *

FLUFFY ROLLS
Ingredients and Directions
Mix together 1/2 cup warm milk, 1/2 cup sugar, 1 teaspoon salt. Dissolve two packets of yeast in 1/2 cup warm water. Stir well. Add to milk mixture. Add two slightly beaten eggs, 1/2 cup shortening, 4 to 5 cups of flour. Mix with spoon, then hand. Turn out onto floured board and knead. Place in greased bowl and turn once. Cover with damp cloth and let rise in warm spot until doubled, about 90

minutes. Punch down and let rise again until almost doubled, about 40 minutes. Divide dough into two. Use half to form 12 balls for plain rolls. Bake at 375 degrees for 25 minutes or until golden brown. Use other half to make sticky buns.

* * *

STICKY BUNS

Roll dough (see above recipe) into oblong and spread with 2 tablespoons of melted butter and sprinkle with 1/2 cup sugar, 1 tablespoon cinnamon, 1/2 cup of chopped walnuts. Roll up and pinch edges together. Cover and let rise until double, about 40 minutes. Slice and place slices in baking pan coated with 1/2 cup melted butter and 1/2 cup brown sugar. Mom sometimes made these with pecans, more often with walnuts. Bake at 375 degrees for 25 minutes or until golden brown. Check with knife to make sure interior of bun is cooked. Turn over at once onto large tray or platter, allowing pan to remain for a minute or so, so butter and sugar will drench buns.

* * *

HAWAIIAN LEMON PIE

Recipes for apple and blackberry pies can be found in most general cookbooks so asserting my rights as compiler to decide which of Mom's pies should conclude this section, I settled on this wonderful favorite. I don't know as it ever went on a picnic with us, but it graced our table many times. Again, I wrote Mom and requested the recipe after I was married, and have it preserved in her handwriting.

Ingredients
3/4 cup sugar
5 tablespoons cornstarch
1/2 teaspoon salt
1 No. 2 can pineapple juice (20 ounces or 2 1/2 cups)
Rind and juice of one lemon
3 egg yolks
2 tablespoons of butter

Directions

In saucepan blend sugar, corn starch and salt. Blend in pineapple juice. Cook, stirring constantly until mixture boils. Beat egg yolks slightly . Add small amount of pie filling to yolks and return all to pan and cook until it boils about 2 minutes. Stir constantly. Remove from heat, add butter, lemon juice and rind and let cool to room temperature. Pour into baked cooled pie crust. Make meringue of 3 egg whites, 6 tablespoons of sugar, dash of salt. Beat until peaks stand up. Place on top of pie and bake at 325 degrees for 25 minutes.

Madeline and Mom put finishing touches on holiday dinner in Roulette at Gram's house.

Terse Verse

UPON FINDING COPIES OF
STEPHEN KING'S BEST SELLING BOOK,
"ON WRITING", IN THE DOLLAR STORE

It's not the bad review I fear
Nor does rejection bring a tear
(well not many).
The spectre that haunts me evermore
is winding up in the dollar store.
But, on the other hand you see,
I'd be in such good companee.
(Previously unpublished)

BIRDIE IN THE BACKYARD
Birdie in the backyard,
Birdie on the fence,
I will sell him to you
for five and twenty cents.

First you have to catch him.
I will tell you how.
Sprinkle salt right on his tail.
Hurry, do it now!

Creep quietly behind him,
SHH!
Make sure you are not heard.
#$%^&^%$#!
What kind of cat are you?
That cannot catch a bird!

And finally to conclude this book with those who light up our lives

THERE ARE BEARS UPSTAIRS

There are bears upstairs, my sister said,
Bears in the closets and under the bed
Bears in the hallway and behind the door
Bears that growl and bears that roar.

She fixed me with a fiendish eye
To see if she could make me cry.
I knew exactly what to do
Just tell myself it wasn't true.

There are no bears upstairs, I said.
No bears in the closet, or under the bed
No bears in the hallway or behind the door
No bears that growl or bears that roar.

My sister smiled and hugged the cat.
"Oh, nooo? Don't be too sure of that."
Her voice was smooth, as smooth as jelly
Butterflies erupted in my belly.

I quivered and quaked;I shook and shrieked.
"Stop that nonsense!" Mom was piqued.
This house is nothing but a zoo.
Go get ready for school, you two.

ZOO, DID SHE SAY ZOO???!!

"Don't make me go upstairs," I pleaded
Shoes in school are seldom needed.
I'll wear my jammies to school today
And comb my cowlick on the way.

But Mom shook her head no, no
So facing an outcome full of woe

And filled with fear and dire doom
I slowly crept up to my room.

And there I found

Tessa Bear and Quinny Bear jumping on the beds
Austin Bear and Riley Bear standing on their heads
Sammy Bear and Maggie Bear playing movie stars
A.J. Bear and Piercey Bear strumming their guitars

I breathed a sigh of great relief
Not a chance I'd come to grief
Oh, teddy dears, such first-rate fun,
I'll play with you when school is done

My Favorite Recipes